Welcome to STBC!

# A

The Supernatural Power

*of* God

## Apostle Ese Duke

# Dedication

First and foremost, I dedicate this book to the precious Holy Spirit, my best friend, senior partner, and my guide who has placed a special anointing upon my life, which has transformed me forever.

I also dedicate this book to the faithful and committed members of Spirit Temple Bible Church Worldwide for their continual support and encouragement to convert my teachings into a book.

And finally, I dedicate this book to my loving and supportive wife, Reverend Gladys Duke and to all my children for their understanding and support of my mandate from God.

# Contents

# Acknowledgement

I acknowledge the Father of our Lord Jesus Christ, our King Jesus and the precious Holy Spirit for the grace to make this book a reality.

Special thanks to all those who contributed their time, resources, and talents in editing and printing this manuscript. Without you this would not have been a completed master-piece. May God bless you tremendously and send destiny helpers at every phase of your life journey in Jesus' name.

# $\mathcal{I}$ntroduction

$\mathcal{Y}$ou may have heard that God does not look at our abilities; He looks at our availability. While that is true, it is only half of the story. The other half is that God puts His ability in you to do His work. It is a powerful, supernatural ability we receive called the anointing. However, before I go into depth about the anointing of the Holy Ghost, it is important to discuss the person of the Holy Spirit. It is vital to understand who He is, what He does, and His role in our lives. Every Christian needs to know Him and not just about Him because ignorance brings limitation to our lives.

This study of the Holy Spirit is designed not only to enhance your knowledge of who He is universally but for you to experience His transforming power and presence in your everyday personal life. So who is this Holy Spirit? What can He do for you?

The anointing of the Holy Spirit is the ability God gives mortal man to do supernatural things for Him. It is a fundamental aspect of the Christian walk God expects all His children to experience. He wants every believer in Christ to be anointed to do His work. The truth is, if you are doing God's work without the anointing, you are headed for trouble.

Do you want to experience more spiritual power in your life? Do you want to break the yokes and bondage in your life and those around you? Are you tired and frustrated with the old routine of going to church with the narration of the power of God without the demonstration of the power? If the answer to these questions is yes, you have the right book in your hands. As you continue to read these pages, God will do something amazing in you.

In this book you will discover:

- What the anointing is
- How the anointing within functions and grows
- The difference between the anointing within and the anointing upon.
- The authority that the anointing within has.
- The two laws operating the anointing within
- How to release the anointing within.
- The levels and dimensions of the anointing
- And many more impactful, life-changing teachings

# Chapter 1
## Who Is the Holy Spirit?

The Holy Spirit is the third person of the Trinity. He proceeded from God. Note the personal pronoun "He," which indicates we are talking primarily about a person. That is to say, the Holy Spirit is a person, not a thing or an active force. Unfortunately, many have the misguided impression that the Holy Spirit is a dove because at Jesus' baptism, "The Spirit of God descended like a dove." Here, you must pay attention to the word "like," which makes a comparison of the Holy Spirit's descension to that of a dove. It does not compare the Holy Spirit to a dove. Thus, it is not referring to what the Holy Spirit looked like but the manner of the descent of the Holy Spirit upon Jesus.

> And Jesus, when he was baptized, went up straightway out of the water: and, lo, the heavens were opened unto him, and he saw the Spirit of God descending like a dove, and lighting upon him (Matthew 3:16).

When you are born again, you are baptized by the Holy Spirit into the body of Christ. The baptism prepares you as the temple of the Holy Spirit for the infilling of the Holy Spirit.

1

He begins the work in and through you. You receive the Spirit of God without measure. However, if you fail to believe God and trust in all of His Word, you limit the Spirit in your life and measure the Spirit to yourself.

> For he whom God hath sent speaketh the words of God: for God giveth not the Spirit by measure unto him (John 3:34).

Jesus received the Holy Spirit without measure. He was sent by God the Father.

> Then said Jesus to them again, Peace be unto you: as my Father hath sent me, even so send I you (John 20:21).

We too have received the Spirit without measure and have been sent by Jesus.

> In the last day, that great day of the feast, Jesus stood and cried, saying, If any man thirst, let him come unto me, and drink.
>
> He that believeth on me, as the scripture hath said, out of his belly shall flow rivers of living water.
>
> But this spake he of the Spirit, which they that believe on him should receive: for the Holy Ghost was not yet given; because that Jesus was not yet glorified (John 7:37–39).
>
> And I will pray the Father, and he shall give you another Comforter, that he may abide with you forever;

> Even the Spirit of truth; whom the world cannot receive, because it seeth him not, neither knoweth him: but ye know him; for he dwelleth with you, and shall be in you.
>
> I will not leave you comfortless: I will come to you (John 14:16–20).

In Greek the two words used for the word "another" are *allos* and *heteros*. Allos means one of the same kind. Heteros means one of a different kind.

The Word "Comforter" in Greek is *Paracletus* – one to walk alongside. Jesus said He will send us allos Paracletus. He said He will not leave us comfortless. In other words, He will not leave us as orphans. There are seven words used to describe this word in the English language to give us clarity on the Holy Spirit – Paracletus.

> And I will ask the Father, and He will give you another Comforter (Counselor, Helper, Intercessor, Advocate, Strengthener, and Standby), that He may remain with you forever—
>
> The Spirit of Truth, Whom the world cannot receive (welcome, take to its heart), because it does not see Him or know and recognize Him. But you know and recognize Him, for He lives with you [constantly] and will be in you.
>
> I will not leave you as orphans [comfortless, desolate, bereaved, forlorn, helpless]; I will come [back] to you (John 14:16–18, Amplified Version).

## Comforter

The Holy Spirit is your Comforter. He is your Father. In your times of sorrow and distress, He will comfort you. When you lose your loved ones to death, divorce or otherwise, He will give you ease and freedom from the pain. If you are distressed because you think you have lost a lot in your life whether financially, emotionally, physically or spiritually, He will restore and comfort you.

> And I will restore to you the years that the locust hath eaten, the cankerworm, and the caterpillar, and the palmerworm, my great army which I sent among you (Joel 2:25).

Not only will He restore your lost material possessions, He will restore your lost time. What do I mean by that? I am talking about acceleration – a rapid realization of what you should have accomplished in the prior years. The things you wanted to acquire and achieve will become possible in a few weeks or months. He will restore your relationships, finances, health, and so forth.

With the Holy Spirit in your life, there is never a too late occurrence. For example, when Lazarus died, his sisters, Mary and Martha thought it was too late for Jesus to do anything to restore his life. The fact is that Lazarus was dead and buried for about three days. However, Jesus is never late and so, He did what seemed impossible. He raised Lazarus from the dead (see John Chapter 11).

## Counselor

> And thine ears shall hear a word behind thee, saying, This is the way, walk ye in it, when ye

turn to the right hand, and when ye turn to the left (Isaiah 30:21).

The Holy Spirit will give you good counsel. He tells you what to do and how to go about it. When you miss your way, He will redirect you. Moreover, you can be certain He will always give you the right advice.

## Advocate

He is our Advocate. He represents us. He is our spokesperson. He is our crusader and adviser. The Holy Spirit will speak on your behalf. He knows all things and is also called the Spirit of Wisdom; hence, the perfect representative in your times of need.

## Intercessor

> Likewise the Spirit also helpeth our infirmities: for we know not what we should pray for as we ought: but the Spirit itself maketh intercession for us with groanings which cannot be uttered.
>
> And he that searcheth the hearts knoweth what is the mind of the Spirit, because he maketh intercession for the saints according to the will of God.

And we know that all things work together for good to them that love God, to them who are the called according to his purpose (Romans 8:26–28).

The Holy Spirit will intercede for you with groanings that cannot be uttered. There are no disappointments or disadvantages for a child of God. All things will always work for your good because the Holy Spirit intercedes for you even in your most dire circumstances. He has made us masters over life and overcomers over all of life's challenges. Even when you don't know what to pray or how to pray, He will negotiate on your behalf.

## Helper

The Holy Spirit will make life easy for you. He is your helper and support. You can depend on Him in all of life's situations. In your education, He will help you. In your relationships, He will help you. You will never be defeated or stranded in life because of the certain help the Holy Spirit gives.

## Strength

As you speak in tongues, the Holy Spirit energizes you. If you are weak physically or spiritually, He will strengthen you. The Bible says that the Holy Spirit will strengthen, reinvigorate, energize, and quicken your mortal body (Romans 8:11).

## Standby

When everything has failed, you have a standby. When education has failed you — you have a standby. When your job has failed you — you have a standby. Even when your local church or her leaders have failed you — the Holy Ghost is your standby. He is like a stand by generator. You are never left without the source of power.

Everyone who has accepted Jesus Christ as Lord and Savior has the anointing within because the Anointed One lives on the inside of him. However, that is different from carrying an anointing upon your life.

We are not anointed to do everything in the kingdom of God. Each of us has an anointing from God to do a particular work. Therefore, you cannot do what someone else does because you feel like it. If you try to step into somebody else's assignment when you do not have the anointing for it, you will struggle. You will find yourself trying to act like the person just because you are excited about what they do, and you feel like doing it. Be warned, if you take that approach in your Christian walk you are setting yourself up for disaster. Trouble is ahead. You need the empowerment of the Holy Spirit.

## The Gifts of the Holy Spirit

We cannot discuss the Holy Spirit without taking a brief look at the gifts of the Spirit and their link to the anointing of the Holy Spirit. There are nine gifts of the Holy Spirit; these nine gifts can be grouped into three categories each containing three gifts: Power gifts, Revelation gifts, and Vocal gifts.

Power Gifts

- Gift of healing
- Gift of working of miracles
- Gift of faith

Revelation Gifts

- Gift of the word of knowledge
- Gift of the word of wisdom
- Gift of discerning of spirits

Vocal Gifts

- Gifts of speaking in tongues (or the gift of tongues)
- Gift of prophecy
- Gift of interpretation of tongues

These nine gifts of the Spirit are given to us as God's children. However, to work in these gifts, we need the anointing of the Holy Spirit. For instance, since I was fourteen years old, I always wanted to operate in the gift of the word of knowledge because my pastor operated in that gift so fluently. I also desired the gift of working of miracles and healings. I prayed for that as a young man. I said, "God, if I can just be like my pastor." Eventually, God answered my prayers. It came to a time in my life I realized that God had given me the opportunity and privilege to operate in the gift of word of knowledge, the gift of word of wisdom, the gift of faith, the gift of healing, and in the gift of miracles.

Often, these gifts will manifest in people differently depending on the will of the Holy Spirit. Usually, the gift of word of knowledge will express itself in my body. What do I mean by that? When I am ministering and someone in the congregation has a back pain, migraine headache or tooth ache, I immediately experience the symptoms of these illnesses in my body. The Holy Spirit prompts me immediately to call out the condition as I feel it. As soon as I call it out and pray for that individual, those symptoms disappear from my body, which is an indication that God healed the person. Now, that is how the gift of the Holy Spirit works in conjunction with God's anointing in our lives.

Sometimes, the Holy Spirit will drop information in my Spirit about someone in the congregation I had no prior knowledge of. The Spirit will give me permission to share that knowledge with the individual and often, that word results in edification and encouragement.

# Chapter 2

## What is the Anointing?

The Anointing is the supernatural power or ability of the Holy Spirit given to a believer to do the work that God has called him or her to do. God's anointing is critical to the manifestation of His power in the world. He does not want us to do His work without the anointing. This is evident as we search the scriptures and see how mighty, notable men of God were able to accomplish their God-given missions.

Aaron and his sons were anointed for the priesthood:

> And thou shalt anoint Aaron and his sons, and consecrate them, that they may minister unto me in the priest's office (Exodus 30:30).

Aaron and his sons were the ones anointed to be priests. Therefore, if any other person or family tried to fill that position, they would have been stepping into unauthorized territory. It didn't matter how popular they were or how much they felt they could do the job. The only thing that mattered was God's anointing.

In Numbers 11:17, we see that Moses carried the anointing of God:

> And I will come down and talk with thee there:
> and I will take of the spirit which is upon thee,
> and will put it upon them; and they shall bear
> the burden of the people with thee, that thou
> bear it not thyself alone.

God anointed Moses as he led the children of Israel to the Promised Land. God took part of that same anointing and put it on other men to assist Moses. Note that these men needed the anointing before they could help Moses deal with the issues the people were facing. They were not just selected and sent. They had to be anointed to do the work.

It's important to note also that God can put the anointing or the spirit of a man of God on your life if you desire and He will. In fact, if you desire, as you read this book, you may also receive the impartation of the anointing from my life upon you. Sometimes, even being in the presence of someone who carries the anointing can cause you to receive the same anointing the person has.

Joshua's anointing was imparted by the laying of hands:

> And Joshua the son of Nun was full of the spirit
> of wisdom; for Moses had laid his hands upon
> him: and the children of Israel hearkened unto
> him, and did as the Lord commanded Moses
> (Deuteronomy 34:9).

We see here that the laying on of hands is not a New Testament phenomenon. It was happening even in Old Testament days. Moses laid his hands on Joshua, and he received the anointing upon his life. The anointing can be transferred by the laying on of hands as commanded by the Lord. The Bible says, "And the children of Israel hearkened unto him, and did as the Lord commanded Moses."

Saul was anointed to be king:

> Then Samuel took a vial of oil, and poured it upon his head, and kissed him, and said, Is it not because the Lord hath anointed thee to be captain over his inheritance? (1 Samuel 10:1).

David was also anointed to be king:

> Then Samuel took the horn of oil, and anointed him in the midst of his brethren: and the Spirit of the Lord came upon David from that day forward. So Samuel rose up, and went to Ramah (1 Samuel 16: 13).

Jesus was anointed to manifest His Lordship:

> How God anointed Jesus of Nazareth with the Holy Ghost and with power: who went about doing good, and healing all that were oppressed of the devil; for God was with him (Act 10:38).

Let me make it very clear: any work that is done for God without His anointing, God rejects. He will not let any man or woman work as His representative without the power of the Holy Spirit. I think it is important for us to read the following scripture:

> And Saul said; bring hither a burnt offering to me, and peace offerings. And he offered the burnt offering.

> And it came to pass, that as soon as he had made an end of offering the burnt offering,

behold, Samuel came; and Saul went out to meet him, that he might salute him.

And Samuel said, What hast thou done? And Saul said, Because I saw that the people were scattered from me, and that thou camest not within the days appointed, and that the Philistines gathered themselves together at Michmash;

Therefore said I, The Philistines will come down now upon me to Gilgal, and I have not made supplication unto the Lord: I forced myself therefore, and offered a burnt offering.

And Samuel said unto Saul thou has done foolishly. Thou has not kept the commandments of the Lord, thy God which He commanded thee for thou would the Lord have established thy kingdom upon Israel for ever.

But now thy kingdom shall not continue: the Lord hath sought him a man after his own heart, and the Lord hath commanded him to be captain over his people, because thou hast not kept that which the Lord commanded thee (1 Samuel 13:9–14).

Saul was anointed as a king, not a priest. Therefore, he was not supposed to do what he did. It was not his office. That's why I tell ministers when someone comes to the altar, don't lay hands on their heads. It's an office. It's a place of authority. You never know what that individual carries that may be transferred to you. Keep your hands to yourself unless God tells you to or unless you know you carry the anointing.

Saul gave God a sacrifice, something good, but it was not his place to do so. God said to Saul, "You know what? Because you did that, I have changed my mind concerning your kingdom. Your kingdom will no more reign forever. You will no longer rule forever. I am now going to give it to David, a man after my own heart."

King Uzziah also tried to be a priest and judgment fell upon him because He did not carry the priestly anointing.

> And they withstood Uzziah the king, and said unto him, It appertaineth not unto thee, Uzziah to burn incense unto the Lord but to the priests, the sons of Aaron, that are consecrated to burn incense: Go out of this sanctuary for thou has trespassed; neither shall it be for thine honour from the Lord God (2 Chronicles 26:18).

Burning incense is like leading in worship. It was a good thing to do; however, King Uzziah was not ordained by God to do that. It was not his place and so he paid a price.

Perhaps, you are involved in a church ministry with people God wants to use, but they don't look qualified. If God has anointed them, it is not in your place to criticize. You may look better, speak better, sing better, dance better, or even be more qualified by the world's standards, but you have no right to criticize God's anointed. It's about the anointing, not the charisma. If God has not given you the anointing to function in that realm, in that place, in that kind of ministry, don't try to fit in. It will not work. You must respect the anointing because the anointing you respect is the anointing you attract.

Doing God's work without the anointing to function removes the protection of God. Do you think I could do what I do and still be able to function well if God doesn't protect me? Impossible! God protects me big time because I am operating within my anointing and territory. He protects my children, wife, businesses, and my cars. Everything is safe and well. Why? Because I am where I'm supposed to be. If I divert and start doing other things that are not within my territory, I am in trouble.

God's anointing is very precious. It is not an earthly commodity but a heavenly one that God puts on the earthly man.

Note the difference between the anointing on you and the anointing in you. All born again Christians have the anointing in them because they have Jesus Christ, the Anointed One, living on the inside. Yes. You are anointed. Why? Because Jesus, the Anointed One resides inside of you. However, even though you have the anointing in you, it doesn't mean it is on you. Having the anointing on you is when God Himself has placed His Spirit on your life and appointed you for a particular function. Remember, the anointing of Saul, Aaron, David, and Jesus was for them to accomplish distinct tasks in the kingdom.

One day, I was preaching and suddenly, I got a note on a piece of paper telling me I had to stop preaching in thirty minutes, I said, "Oh my, I haven't even started preaching yet. How am I going to do all these things? How am I going to preach and still minister to the people?" Their expectations are great whenever I minister. I paused and the Holy Spirit told me, "You know what? That's fine; move. That's okay. Just move." As I moved, I beckoned God and said, "Lord, let it flow." Immediately, the power of God began to flow and things started to happen. Do you know why? The Holy Spirit was already on me. I simply signaled the anointing of God that is upon my life to flow. It was very powerful on that day and in that meeting. We had never experienced that much anointing in the entire audience. The power of God was so strong that almost everybody experienced it as I moved from seat to seat. I hadn't even preached for more than ten minutes.

The anointing of God is precious and holy. That is why God expects consecration before he puts His anointing on you.

> And ye shall not go out of the door of the tabernacle of the congregation in seven days, until the days of your consecration be at an end: for seven days shall he consecrate you.
>
> As he hath done this day, so the Lord hath commanded to do, to make an atonement for you.
>
> Therefore shall ye abide at the door of the tabernacle of the congregation day and night seven days, and keep the charge of the Lord, that ye die not: for so I am commanded.

So Aaron and his sons did all things which the Lord commanded by the hand of Moses (Leviticus 8:33–35).

God's anointing is so precious and holy, Aaron needed to consecrate himself before God placed it on him.

> And Moses said unto Aaron, and unto Eleazar and unto Ithamar, his sons, Uncover not your heads, neither rend your clothes; lest ye die, and lest wrath come upon all the people: but let your brethren, the whole house of Israel, bewail the burning which the Lord hath kindled.
>
> And ye shall not go out from the door of the tabernacle of the congregation, lest ye die: for the anointing oil of the Lord is upon you. And they did according to the word of Moses (Leviticus 10:6–7).

Somebody died in Aaron's family and God told him not to cry. He was instructed not to weep over this dead relative because God's anointing on him at the time was unique.

The anointing might require that you make sacrifices. You may not be able to talk to everybody, eat on Sunday mornings even when you are out of town or hang out with certain people. His anointing can be demanding, but God will always back you up. That's why the Bible says: "Touch not mine anointed." God does not mess with that. Some people say, "I'm anointed. Touch me not." But, that's not referring to the anointing in you; it is referring to the one upon you.

If people try to fight me physically, they would be putting themselves in danger. I may not say a word, but they may have cursed themselves. You must be extremely careful with anyone who carries the anointing. I am not talking about those who say they are anointed, but those who authentically carry the anointing. Many people say they have the anointing but they don't.

How can you identify when you carry the anointing? It has to show. It is like pregnancy. A woman cannot hide the fact that she is pregnant. Everywhere she goes, people know she is carrying new life within her.

The anointing that God places on His vessels is holy. Moses was anointed. Miriam, Moses' sister, was upset because Moses married somebody outside of his race. Miriam had the right to be upset because what Moses did was against the law, and He was well aware he should not have married outside the Jewish race. However, God was upset with Miriam for speaking against and touching His anointed one. He struck her with leprosy. Miriam learned the hard way. We must watch over the servants of God closely. The anointing of God is an interest of God so when God anoints someone, He is interested in that person. Hence, those who are obedient are covered by God.

# Chapter 3

## Purpose of the Anointing

We have all been called to do the work of God. Therefore, all God's children need the anointing upon their lives. Doing God's work does not mean you have to be a preacher in the church. It does not mean you are anointed to be a pastor or to be involved in the fivefold ministry – apostle, prophet, evangelist, pastor or teacher. Rather, it means you are anointed. Therefore, when you go into the supermarket, the hospitals, and wherever you venture to pray for the sick, they will be healed. You can go out there and cast out devils. You can go out there and command cancer to leave somebody's body.

In the Bible, God put His anointing on certain men for all manner of workmanship. Some were anointed to be good craftsmen, tailors, and singers. On the other hand, some were anointed with wisdom; they just knew how to solve problems. Hence, we can see that God's anointing is not only for the pulpit. Every child of God can do miracles. However, when you are anointed to perform miracles, it becomes your lifestyle.

Some time back, God told me that Spirit Temple Bible Church is a special place where His power is released and where His Spirit is manifested. He said I don't have to do anything to try to entice anybody to come to this church.

He brings them in by His Spirit, and He keeps them in by His Spirit. It is neither me nor anyone else.

In the early days of the New Testament church, God added 3,000 people in one day. In other words, within twenty four hours, 3000 souls were saved by His Spirit. Today, God by His own Spirit is bringing men and women into the church. He is building it one layer at a time and putting things in place because something big is about to happen. It is not by might nor by power, but by my Spirit saith the Lord (Zechariah 4:6).

## Impact the World

If we all have God's anointing like the disciples did, can you comprehend the effect we would have? These twelve Holy Ghost-filled men changed the entire world. As a matter of fact, it is said they had such great influence, they turned the world upside down (Acts 17:6). The disciples had no aircraft, sound systems, computers, Internet or email. So why were they so successful? It's not because they spoke eloquently. It's not that they went to large conferences or the best seminaries. No! They had something different in their lives. They were filled with the Holy Ghost and power. They performed great miracles, signs, and wonders.

We have to be hungry for God if we want His power to sweep all over the world. Can you commit your life to pay the price? We must agree to pay the price and don't worry about who gets the credit. It is not about that. It's about getting the job done and bringing souls to the kingdom of God by the anointing of the Holy Ghost. The world is not going to change because of your rich knowledge of the Bible but by the move of the Holy Ghost.

As stated earlier, in the book of Acts, the disciples turned the city upside down. Can you imagine you and I going to a big office, all anointed, and when we step through the door, everyone there is slain under the Spirit? Imagine five hundred of us at a stadium; everybody starts falling under the anointing and getting healed of their sicknesses and diseases. People would say, "Wait a minute; what is going on here? We want what you have." The power of the Holy Spirit would be manifested to them.

> But ye shall receive power, after that the Holy Ghost is come upon you: and ye shall be witnesses unto me both in Jerusalem, and in all Judaea, and in Samaria, and unto the uttermost part of the earth (Acts 1:8).

## To Be Witnesses of Christ

Jesus told the disciples to wait in the upper room and the Holy Ghost would come upon them. Their lives and circumstances would change because of the power received from the Holy Spirit. In fact, they would become His witnesses in Jerusalem, Judea and the uttermost parts of the earth. So when you receive power, you become a witness. What do witnesses do? They testify of what they have seen and heard. They testify of the power of God. What better way to testify than to perform? Do you get it? In court, when the experts testify, many times, they don't talk much; they put on the video clips of the action or show pictures to tell the story, to bear witness. Likewise, as witnesses for Christ with God's anointing – no more talking! Instead, demonstrate what Christ can do and what He has done. He can heal your body and eradicate every demonic operation in your life. The Devil has to listen to the powerful, anointed voices of God's people.

And my speech and my preaching was not with enticing words of man's wisdom, but in demonstration of the Spirit and of power (1 Corinthians 2:4).

## Good Health

You need the anointing upon your life to stop sickness from visiting your home. I can testify that the Enemy once thought he could plague my home with sickness. However, when I received God's anointing, I warned him, "No more can you visit my home." And he has listened to that for years. That includes my children. The Devil cannot make my children sick. I refuse to allow that. At one time in their lives, they would be sick until I realized God's anointing upon my life could be put on them. And so, I decreed that they will be sick no more. From that day, nobody has gone to the hospital. I'm not kidding. The time came when I had to ward off all of the nonsense of going to the hospital every week; that is devilish. Tell yourself, "I will have no need to go to the hospital anymore because I walk in divine health. I am not sick any longer. I will remain healthy. My family will remain healthy. They walk in divine health, in the name of Jesus. No sickness, no disease will afflict us because we are anointed."

Disease can leave your household if you believe it. Life revolves around belief. Keep that in your heart. Now, that is not me talking; that is the Bible. The Bible also says as a man believes in his heart, so he is. If sickness tries to attach itself to your body, you say, "No, no, no, no. Not this body. Come on. Get out of me!" You never speak sickness into existence. If you believe and truly believe, disease can leave your household for good.

Be radical for Christ. Be stubborn for Christ. Sometimes, we are stubborn for the wrong reasons. I believe God. If I die believing, that's it, but I refuse to agree with those symp-toms. I'm going to trust God and believe Him for His greater power.

## Supernatural Works

The enablement and impartation of the anointing will help those who have received it to do supernatural works. If you have faith and believe, you will receive God's anointing upon your life. Notice, this is not for everybody who will read this book but for those who have faith to receive God's anointing upon their lives. That anointing will ward off any calamity and the attacks of the Enemy. The anointing will draw you closer to God as you are consecrated before our Lord Jesus. If you fall into that category, believe that this is your day to receive the impartation of God's anointing on your life. It will keep you where God wants you to be. It will help you to manifest supernatural power.

## Function in the Fivefold Ministry

Those who operate in the gifts of the Holy Spirit and in the fivefold ministry have to possess the anointing to function in the office to which they are called. Just because someone is able to type a Word document does not make that person a secretary. However, every secretary should be able to type a Word document.

So just because somebody can give you a word of proph-ecy does not make that person a prophet. Every Christian should be able to give someone a word of edification and en-couragement. Furthermore, just because somebody opened or planted a church does not make that person an apostle.

It is critical to talk about the anointing of the Holy Spirit because all of the offices of the fivefold ministry, can only function properly when you understand how it works. Some people have lots of charisma but no power. They can be very eloquent in speech, but they've got no manifestation of the power of God.

The anointing is the power of God working through a person, and you cannot deny its existence because it is very visible and tangible to those around you. The anointing (the power of God) is different from the presence of the Holy Spirit. Every born again believer has the presence of the Holy Spirit and the anointing of God on the inside of them.

## Carry the Seven Manifestations of the Spirit

> And there shall come forth a rod out of the stem of Jesse, and a Branch shall grow out of his roots:

> And the spirit of the Lord shall rest upon him, the spirit of wisdom and understanding, the spirit of counsel and might, the spirit of knowledge and of the fear of the Lord (Isaiah 11:1–2).

Contained in these verses are the seven manifestations of the Holy Spirit, NOT seven spirits:

1. The Spirit of the Lord
2. The Spirit of wisdom
3. The Spirit of understanding
4. The Spirit of counsel
5. The Spirit of might
6. The Spirit of knowledge
7. The Spirit of the fear of the Lord

Jesus had these seven manifestations and so, all the

children of God can also manifest them in their lives. The Spirit of the Lord rested upon Jesus (in reference to the anointing). Even in the womb of Mary, Jesus had the anointing in Him.

> But ye shall receive power, after that the Holy Ghost is come upon you: and ye shall be witnesses unto me both in Jerusalem, and in all Judaea, and in Samaria, and unto the uttermost part of the earth (Acts 1:8).

## Receive Power

The Holy Ghost gives us power. Power rearranges; power gives evidence; power changes circumstances; power gives us light; power helps us cook our meals; power helps wash our clothes, and power helps vacuum our houses, literally. So power is very important, it takes care of a lot of things. As said before, all children of God need power upon them to do the works that God has destined for them to do. The power upon you refers to the anointing of God on your life. God's anointing is the power of God. When the Holy Spirit comes upon you, you receive the anointing upon but when you are born again you receive the anointing within.

> But you have received the Holy Spirit, and he lives within you, so you don't need anyone to teach you what is true. For the Spirit teaches you everything you need to know, and what he teaches is true—it is not a lie. So just as he has taught you, remain in fellowship with Christ (1 John 2:27, NLT).

This Scripture is not saying that you don't need a teacher,

what it's saying in the NLT is that the Holy Spirit, the anointing of God is in you and it will tell you what is true or not true. It will keep you away from error and deception. But let's look at the King James Version.

> But the anointing which ye have received of him abideth in you, and ye need not that any man teach you: but as the same anointing teacheth you of all things, and is truth, and is no lie, and even as it hath taught you, ye shall abide in him (1 John 2:27).

In King James Version it says but the anointing, which ye have received of Him, the Holy Spirit abideth "in you."

I read those two translations to help you understand the words the "anointing" and the "Holy Spirit" in this instance are synonymous. That way, you will understand what this verse is talking about. In NLT, we read about the Holy Spirit but in the King James Version, it says the anointing within you.

## For Discernment

If you have the anointing within, you can discern if someone tries to deceive you with a word saying, "Thus saith the Lord." You will know because the anointing within reveals to you that whatever the person is saying does not line up with the Bible. As I often say to those who spend one-on-one time with me, be very watchful of anyone who comes to you saying he or she is a prophet and can tell you your future. Run away! Ministers of God don't need to announce the office they are in. Their gifts speak for themselves. Beware! That person is introducing him or herself as a prophet, pastor, apostle or otherwise, to catch your attention. They want you to listen.

Those who are gullible will say, "Please, tell me what the Lord is telling you. Tell me something."

People have come to me saying, "Pastor, please, tell me something. Tell me something right now." But I say, "No. We don't do it like that." I wasn't created to tell everybody something. I would often ask, "What is God telling you? You tell me what God is telling you." They would respond, "No, He is not talking to me." I tell them, "He is talking to you; you are just not listening." I always encourage people to listen to God. Otherwise, they become too dependent on calling the prophet to, "Tell me something."

If you are a prophet, a pastor or whatever office you hold and someone tells you, "Please, tell me something. What is God telling you?" tell them, "He is talking to you too. What are you sensing in your spirit?" Encourage them to listen. Let them know they may not be hearing because they are not listening or they are talking too much. Don't tell them what The Lord has not told you. God has not put you in an office to give every person a word.

# Chapter 4

## Three Realms of the Supernatural

Talking about the anointing of the Spirit is delving into God's realm of the supernatural. Your connection to this realm unleashes the power of God in your life and ministry. There are three realms of the supernatural:

1. The Realm of Faith
2. The Realm of the Anointing
3. The Realm of Glory

### The Realm of Faith

The entry level to the realm of the supernatural is the realm of faith. We know that faith is the substance of things hoped for, the evidence of things not yet seen (Hebrews 11:1). Faith is very important; you cannot operate in the anointing without it. So faith is the legal entrance into the realm of the supernatural. Let's go a little deeper. Faith is what is needed to pull what is in the realm of the spirit into the physical realm so it is manifested. In other words, faith is pulling something from the expanded state into a solid state. To flow in the anointing, you must understand the work of faith because without faith, you cannot accomplish anything with God.

Faith is very important, and we've been taught that it comes by hearing the Word of God. On the other hand, fear comes by hearing the words of the Devil or words contrary to the Word of God. So, importantly, if you desire to operate in the anointing, you must watch who you are listening to. This is significant because the anointing of God cannot really flow in your life if you don't watch who and what you are hearing. If your faith level decreases, the anointing will not flow. That's why many men and women who function in the anointing have different lifestyles. They don't go everywhere; they don't listen to everything; they don't have too many friends who do not flow in the power of God. They are very careful about where they go and who they hang out with. They are well aware that the anointing is a heavenly, tangible, special commodity. It's not cheap. There is a heavy price to pay to receive it.

If you only knew what some of us had to give up in our lives just to stand in the offices to which God called us. We didn't acquire the ability to operate in the anointing anywhere and anytime by happenstance. It did not occur because we felt like it. It happened after making certain lifestyle choices, major sacrifices, and earnestly desiring the Spirit of God.

> And Jesus being full of the Holy Ghost returned from Jordan, and was led by the Spirit into the wilderness,
>
> Being forty days tempted of the devil. And in those days he did eat nothing: and when they were ended, he afterward hungered (Luke 4:1–2).

> And Jesus returned in the power of the Spirit into Galilee: and there went out a fame of him through all the region round about (Luke 4:14).

What was Jesus' secret to power? It's found in the verses between Luke 4:2 and Luke 4:14. The events of verse fourteen would not have occurred if verse three to thirteen did not take place . Jesus went into the wilderness and then suddenly, He came out full of power. Something special happened in the wilderness. He received the anointing. Do you want the anointing of God in your life? As God's children, we need to have God's power manifesting in our lives because it is a major witness for His kingdom. There was a time that God sent Moses to lead His people, the Israelites, out of the land of Egypt. Moses, filled with fear and trepidation stuttered, "But God, these guys won't believe that you sent me. I mean they won't believe me."

God said, "Listen, I am going to give you something."

> And Moses answered and said, But, behold, they will not believe me, nor hearken unto my voice: for they will say, The Lord hath not appeared unto thee.
>
> And the Lord said unto him, What is that in thine hand? And he said, A rod.
>
> And he said, Cast it on the ground. And he cast it on the ground, and it became a serpent; and Moses fled from before it.
>
> And the Lord said unto Moses, Put forth thine hand, and take it by the tail. And he put forth

his hand, and caught it, and it became a rod in his hand:

That they may believe that the Lord God of their fathers, the God of Abraham, the God of Isaac, and the God of Jacob, hath appeared unto thee.

And the Lord said furthermore unto him, Put now thine hand into thy bosom. And he put his hand into his bosom: and when he took it out, behold, his hand was leprous as snow.

And he said, Put thine hand into thy bosom again. And he put his hand into his bosom again; and plucked it out of his bosom, and, behold, it was turned again as his other flesh.

And it shall come to pass, if they will not believe thee, neither hearken to the voice of the first sign, that they will believe the voice of the latter sign.

And it shall come to pass, if they will not believe also these two signs, neither hearken unto thy voice, that thou shalt take of the water of the river, and pour it upon the dry land: and the water which thou takest out of the river shall become blood upon the dry land (Exodus 4:1–9).

Moses said, "But God, how? Can I just go like that without any evidence?"

And God replied, "What is in your hand?"

And Moses said, "A rod."

God said, "Throw the rod down."

These days, when many of us see things happen in the church, we think they are new events, but they are not. God has been manifesting Himself in various ways from the beginning of time. You may see many things happening in the churches that you think are odd, but they are not. God told Moses to throw the rod down. That seemed like a strange instruction. What could a simple shepherd's staff do? But Moses was obedient. What happened to the rod? It turned into a serpent. What would you think if that happened in your church? "What's going on here? What's happening here? Pastor just threw the microphone down and it turned into a serpent."

What was Moses' response when the rod turned into a serpent? He was scared. The first experience of the anointing upon your life will shock you. You will be extremely surprised. You will say, "Wow, this stuff is different." The anointing changes your life completely.

Moses fled from the serpent. How can a rod become a serpent? Adding more oddity to the situation, God told Moses, "Take it by the tail." Moses took the serpent by the tail, and suddenly, that serpent returned to being a rod. Since then, it was called the rod of God.

God then told Moses, "Now put your hand in your pocket. Bring it out." Moses brought his hand out, and it was as white as a leper. God told him, "Put it back in your pocket again." Moses obeyed and when he brought it back out it was clean — signs and wonders.

> The world we live in today is looking for the manifestation of the power of God. Many are tired of people just quoting the Bible and talking without the revelation of power. They are tired of people saying, "The power of God moved in

Wales or Azusa about one hundred years ago." How about you? With the anointing of God on your life, you too can impact the world. You have the same grace on your life. The world is looking for evidence of God's power to be drawn to the gospel of Christ. If we must reach the regions of the world for God, every one of us needs to start walking in that power.

Imagine you prayed for somebody or maybe, you just went to minister to someone and the power of God hit that place. The people there would say, "Wait a minute. Who are you?" And when you tell them, "Come to my church," they will come with you. In fact, when they see you demonstrate God's power, they will not hesitate to say, "I'm going to that place." They will give their lives to Jesus quickly because they see real power. However, if you are like them with the same struggles, problems, and complaints, why should they follow you?

Think about the disciples of Christ before they had God's anointing upon them. They could not win anyone to Christ. Peter was always talking, but the results were not forthcoming. However, the moment they were anointed, one speech, brought thousands to Christ. 3,000 people were saved just like that because of the anointing. The anointing made the difference. When you speak under the anointing, anything can happen. The next time the disciples spoke 5,000 people were added. The anointing of God brings growth. If we take time to tell people what we are experiencing in a church with the anointing, and what God is doing, it will spread and the church will be packed in less than a month because the anointing of God attracts.

People are looking to see where God is moving now, not where God moved. Who wants to live in the past? I want to live in the now, where God is moving now, not where He used to move. So God's anointing is very important and the church should "catch" the anointing. After it is caught, it is taught.

You catch it. You can do all the teaching but if you don't catch it in your spirit, you just have head knowledge. However, it cannot manifest in your life because you've not caught it yet. So you have to open your spirit to catch it. Once you catch the anointing, that's it. Are you ready to catch the anointing? After you've caught it, you begin to study it. Your eyes start to open because you have already caught it. Trying to study so you can have it doesn't work. It's when you have caught that anointing of God upon your life that things begin to happen.

## The Realm of the Anointing

The second realm of the supernatural is the anointing. Like I said earlier, in this context, the anointing is basically God working through man. The anointing of God is very important and every child of God should hunger for it. Many Christians may not understand this, but God's anointing is within you to do great work in your life if you know how. It can do miraculous things when activated and stirred up.

The anointing within is in your spirit man. Praying in tongues stirs it up. The way to see the manifestation of God's anointing and His gifts in your life is praying in the Spirit. When you stir up the anointing of God in your life that is in you, not upon you, that anointing operates from your inner man.

The Spirit of God resides in that inner man, which is the Holy of Holies. When you begin to stir up the anointing, it goes from the Holies of Holies to the holy place, which is your soul. When you keep on stirring it up, it goes to the outer court, which is your physical body. So whatever was happening in your soulish realm, the more you stir up the anointing of God within you, the more your soulish realm, your mind and your emotions align with your Spirit.

If the Spirit that raised Christ from the dead dwells in you, that same spirit can quicken your outer court. It will quicken the outer court or your mortal body (Romans 8:11). So the anointing within, which you received in the instant you were born again, is the most important anointing. Now, if the working of the anointing within you is not properly understood, and you have the anointing upon you, but it is not checked by the anointing within, you can go astray. Therefore, you must understand how the anointing works within you. Needless to say, the anointing that comes upon you is equally important. Without it, you can do little to change your world.

The Bible says that God is able to do abundantly above all that we can ask or think according to that anointing that works in you. The anointing that works in you can do several things. It helps, guides, and keeps you healthy if you understand how it works. If you understand the working of that anointing within, you can release it for your physical, spiritual, and emotional wellbeing.

The anointing upon you is not for you. It's for those to whom you minister and to do things outside of you. It's like putting on a jacket. You wear it on the exterior. Its intensity increases and decreases depending on many factors, which I will share with you. It is important to understand that the anointing that is upon you is for service. In other words, it equips you with whatever you need to serve efficiently and effectively in the kingdom. Whereas the anointing within you is for your spiritual growth and for you to be all God has destined.

The anointing upon you is necessary for successful ministerial work. Without the anointing upon you, no matter how hard you try, you will struggle. However, once you receive that anointing upon your life and whatever you touch will prosper.

All Christians should know it is very important to have God's anointing upon our lives. It's very important because that anointing upon your life can do tremendous work. It can take you to a place you only imagined. The anointing upon you will set the captives free. You will be empowered to tell the demon, "Leave now!" The Devil will know you carry that authority. For example, if a police officer wearing regular clothing approaches you and says, "Don't get into your car," you may not pay attention to what he is saying. But if he wears his police uniform or jacket and he tells you the same thing, your response will be different. You will have to pay attention to his instruction because of the visible uniform he is wearing. His uniform is a symbol of the authority he has. Similarly, the anointing, your jacket, is a representation of the authority God has given you to defeat the Devil.

It's unfortunate that many Christians are ignorant of the "anointing upon" and what it represents. Yet, the Devil understands it very well. He was an anointed cherub. He knows what the anointing is. He knows how it operates. He knows the power of the "anointing upon," and he has deceived a lot of God's people not to walk in that anointing.

Within the anointing, there are three levels. I will simply give an overview here but I will deal with these in more depth later. We have what we call the "lepers anointing," which refers to the anointing you receive at salvation. That is basically the anointing within. It is also known as the "believers anointing."

Then you have the "priestly anointing" also known as the ministerial anointing, which is the anointing for service. This anointing is also referred to as the "anointing upon," which we discussed previously. The third one is what the Bible refers to as the kingly anointing (1 Samuel 10:1), which is another level of God's anointing upon your life. It is different from the priestly anointing. The kingly anointing is an anointing of a dominion where you dominate your dominators. When you say something, the Devil has no choice but to bow.

## The Realm of Glory

The third and highest level of the supernatural realm is the glory of God. Glory is the manifest presence of God. It is the atmosphere of heaven. This is God's presence manifesting in the physical form and tangibly. It is God doing His work and operating according to His sovereignty and initiatives. God does what He does without the use of a man but it is still initiated by hunger for the glory of the Lord. The glory is the high mark of the supernatural living for a child of God.

The presence of God is not the same as the power of God. Until you know the difference between the glory and the anointing, you will miss out as a child of God. God wants you not only to walk by faith but also to operate in the anointing and to live in His glory. For more on His glory please refer to the book, *The Presence of God* by same author.

# Chapter 5

## New Levels of the Anointing

There are different levels of the anointing. One time I told God, "You know what? If this work has to start in Allentown then there has to be a next level."

I have been in ministry for many years, and I have preached in different places. I've seen God moved in my life at different times when I ministered in various places. I've always noticed when I preached elsewhere, His anointing was powerful, but when I went back home, I returned to the way I was – less potent. I said, "God, this thing must be consistent." At that time, I understood the anointing to a degree so I knew I could also flow in the anointing in the house of God. Nobody knows that you don't carry that much of it. If someone ministers in your church and the anointing of healing is there, that minister can flow in healing if he/she has the faith to do so. This is because the house flows in the anointing.

One day, I was preaching in a church in Baltimore. A highly anointed psalmist ministered in song prior. I was supposed to speak immediately after her. I knew that if I could move in that flow, mighty works would follow. The pastor told me, "Wait; let's take offering." I said, "No, don't do offering yet. Let me just minister first" because I knew if they took the offering at that time, they would dampen the entire service.

I wanted to just jump in the same anointing. In fact, once I grabbed the microphone, instantly, miracles began to take place everywhere in the congregation. The power of God was so strong, everybody was under the anointing. People kept falling as I walked past them.

I returned to my church thinking I was going to do the same thing there, but I was wrong. "Oh, my goodness, what happened to me?" At that time, I was anointed, but at a different level of anointing. However, some years ago, the Lord decided to make the power in me permanent.

On that day, I had been fasting and praying for months. I prayed earnestly, "God, I want more." I just kept on saying, "God, you have to do something. I cannot pastor this church in Allentown like any other person. Something must be different. I'm not just going to preach and give a nice sermon when people come to church." I said, "I want to see your power manifest." I did that for months and months and months.

We had just started the ministry at the time, about three months. Miracles were taking place in the church, but the full power of God was not evident. Until one day, I was in my car praying. I was constantly praying. In fact, at that time, if my wife called me on the phone, I would say, "Please, I'm sorry. I can't talk much right now. I'm talking to the Holy Ghost. Excuse me." That's the way it was for months. I would not take calls from a lot of people and if I did, they were very short because I didn't want to miss my communion with the Holy Spirit. I did the same thing at home.

One day, as I was driving back from Reading, very close to a place in Topton, PA. I was praying on the phone with one of my friends from Nigeria whom I had known since I was the age of 14. As I prayed fervently, suddenly, the anointing of God hit me so strongly, I had to pull my car to the side of the road. My hands were on fire. My body was frozen. The anointing was so strong I wept uncontrollably. I was sobbing and saying, "God, that is enough." I couldn't move my left hand because of the power of the anointing. In fact, you would think I had fallen ill in the car, but I knew what was going on. I knew something supernatural had happened.

I couldn't wait to get home to try it out. On arrival, I called my wife and children. I called everybody, "Come; let me check this out. Something happened to me in the car." They all came. I started laying hands on them to see if this thing was real. As I laid hands on them, the power of God kept hitting them. Suddenly, everybody started laughing uncontrollably. I was laughing; they were laughing, and we were falling down. I said, "Okay, I am going to try it on Sunday."

So I went to church on Sunday, and I was pacing back and forth saying, "Oh, my God, this thing better work now." I told the people, "Today, God is going to touch every one of you." Everybody lined up waiting for what would happen next because we had never seen anything like that before. So I was just saying, "Let me just pray for somebody." I didn't feel anything. I felt something in the car. I felt something in the house, but in the church, I felt nothing. I said, "What is going on here?" So I went ahead, and I just reluctantly touched the first person. She fell as if she had been shocked with electricity. At that time, there were no catchers. I laid my hands on the next person and to the floor she fell. My faith grew. I kept going and everybody in that particular service received the touch of God.

I went to one corner of the meeting room towards the door, and I realized that when I got close to the door, I could not stand because the power of God was very strong there. When I moved away from the door, I could stand but when I went near, I could not stand. My legs were like jelly in that place, but I was enjoying myself there too. The men had to hold me up. They did not know what to do with me. The power of God intensified. We were all learning how the anointing works.

I began to see that there is, truthfully, something called the power of God in the life of believers. Everything just changed. Within a couple of months, we moved from that place. God was moving so mightily. During that period, somebody was raised from the dead at the Lehigh Valley Hospital. A young man, nineteen years old at the time, came out of a coma. This young boy was literally dead because he was not breathing. We went to the hospital, lay hands on him, and God supernaturally brought his dead body to life. So the anointing makes a difference. It brings increase and manifestations.

One day at church during prayer in the kitchen, my leg was burning like fire. I said, "Please, bring me something cold." I was thinking if I put my legs on the metal table, it would get cold, but it didn't. So I asked the people to touch my leg. One brother touched my feet and the power of God hit him just by touching my feet. I said, "Oh, my goodness. This is power here." So everyone started touching my feet and the power of God intensified. You see, once you appreciate the anointing of God, it works in your life. I am sharing this with you because I want you to get hungry for the power of God. What does the power do for you? A lot! It rearranges your life.

God said to me, "My son, I have given you a commodity that people are praying, begging, and crying for. Now, you need to leave everything and just follow me full time." I had to quit my business, my profession. Why? The anointing. Without the anointing, it would have been senseless to leave my medical profession and start pastoring fulltime while renting a place in the Mall.

What gives anyone courage to do God's work? The anointing. Once you have God's anointing on your life, you will never suffer. You will never struggle. You will never beg for bread because anything you touch turns to gold. I pray today as you read this book that God would put that hunger in your spirit. That you will be willing to pay the price because the anointing of God is so sweet. Your life changes completely. So I pray that you will have an increase in the dimension of God's anointing upon your life. Ask God to give you a hunger for His anointing. It brings mighty miracle working ability.

Pray that God will manifest Himself in your life and anoint you afresh.

# Chapter 6

## The Fivefold Ministry

$\mathcal{T}$he fivefold ministry refers to those who have been anointed, not those who call themselves anointed or whom mortal man puts a hand on. A certificate that says a person is an apostle, prophet, evangelist, pastor or teacher does not make him or her one. It does not mean the person is anointed for that office. Just because you went to a Bible College does not make you a pastor. Just because you went to a school of the prophets does not make you a prophet.

There are unique anointings for apostles, pastors, teachers, evangelists, and prophets. The anointing for the fivefold ministry comes with the office. For instance, the office of the president comes with the power of the office of the president and whatever the president says is backed by that office. The president is a human in every sense, but he passes laws and decrees because of the office he holds. Once he sits in that office, he can sign documents into law. That same man you had lunch with previously can change the events of the world and people's lives with the stroke of a pen, simply because of his office.

If somebody calls himself an apostle, there should be evidence of his apostleship – the anointing in his life. A person is not an apostle simply because he loves to call himself an apostle. Instead, an apostle operates in the power gifts and the revelation gifts. You cannot be an apostle without operating in the power gifts – the gift of faith, the gift of working of miracles and the gift of healings. You have to operate in, at least, two of these gifts. You also have to operate in the revelation gifts – the gift of prophecy, the gift of the word of knowledge or the gift of the word of wisdom. Additionally, you have to operate in the vocal gift. You are not an apostle because you started a church last week or because you just believe or feel you're an apostle. It doesn't work by feelings. If those things are not in your life, you are not in the office yet so sit down. Don't destroy yourself. When you begin to manifest and see manifestations of the gift of God and His anointing upon your life, you know you can function in that office as an apostle.

## Office of the Prophets

In the office of a prophet, you must operate in the revelation gifts. That means you cannot be a prophet without having the revelation gifts – gift of prophecy, the gift of word of knowledge, and the gift of the word of wisdom. To be a prophet, one must also operate in, at least, one or two of the vocal gifts – the gift of speaking in tongues or the gift of interpretation of tongues. The point is you cannot call yourself a prophet because somebody said, "From now on, you are a prophet" and so you walk around saying, "Yeah, last week, somebody told me I'm a prophet, so I'm a prophet." Your ability to prophesy does not make you a prophet either.

The church of God needs to get this because there are nine other ministry gifts and in them is a gift called the gift of the prophesying believer. Every believer can prophesy. Prophesy to yourself every morning. Speak God's Word into your life. However, because you prophesy to yourself does not mean you have the office of a prophet.

## The Office of the Evangelist and Pastor

The same applies to being an evangelist. An evangelist has the power gifts and also the gift of teaching. A pastor has to have the vocal gifts, the teaching gifts, and also the administration gifts. These are very important.

## The Office of the Teacher

Teachers, on the other hand, must have the gift of divine revelation where God reveals things to them as they read the Word of God. His divine revelation enables them to present God's Word in such a way that even a little child can understand.

Not every Christian is in the fivefold ministry. So when you see somebody operating within an office, that anointing comes with that office. You may try the same thing and it may not work. Don't kill yourself; they have been called by God to function in that office. Consequently, whatever they say comes to pass. Don't try to be who you are not. If you don't have that anointing in your life, and you are trying to be who you are not, you will destroy yourself and others.

It is important to lay the foundation of the anointing because many people want the anointing but don't understand its purpose. God does not give the anointing for you to become pious and self-righteous. He doesn't give it for you to think you know it all and have arrived. You have a lot to learn. Don't think because you have laid hands on a blind person and he received his sight, you should start your church. If you don't carry that anointing, it will be very stressful. That's why some pastors are under so much stress and tension.

They work and work and work and work and work and pray and fast and pray and pray; yet, nothing changes. Then they blame the members. They say, "There is an Achan in the house. There's somebody here who is stopping things from working." But that's not the reason. It's because they are not in the right office. If you are operating in your God-ordained office, it's easy to function. Your ministry is active and great things happen.

Have you ever been in a meeting organized by an evangelist? Did you notice sometimes the crowd is so large that people have to wait in long lines to hear the evangelist? It's the anointing that draws the people to the meetings. Those evangelists have God's anointing on their lives. Some evangelists cannot preach good messages; they are not eloquent, but they have the anointing.

## *Wait until the anointing rests on you before you take off.*

I have seen a lot of believers struggled in their lives because they acted on their own volition. They say, "The Lord is telling me to start a church somewhere next door to you." They take several members of your church and started their church. They ended up with no members because the ones they took left them and nobody joined. The person feels ashamed to return to the original church so he walks around saying, "I am a traveling evangelist. I am a blessing to the body of Christ. I go to different churches every day of the week to express my gift." The truth is they have lost their bearings.

## The Nine Gifts of the Spirit

> But the manifestation of the Spirit is given to every man to profit withal.
>
> For one is given by the Spirit the word of wisdom, to another the word of knowledge by the same Spirit.
>
> To another faith by the same Spirit; to another the gifts of healing by the same Spirit.
>
> To another, working of miracles; to another prophecy; to another, discerning of spirits; to another divers kinds of tongues; to another the interpretation of tongues.
>
> But all of these worketh that one and the selfsame Spirit, dividing to every man severally as he will (1 Corinthians 12:7–11).

You need God's special anointing to operate in the gifts mentioned in the verse above. Every child of God can receive this special anointing to operate in these gifts, it's not necessary to fake it.

## Help and Administration

Some believers are anointed to be deacons, administrators, and to do special work. And they do it with much ease.

> And God hath set some in the church, first apostles, secondarily prophets, thirdly teachers, after that miracles, then gifts of healings,

helps, governments, diversities of tongues (1 Corinthians 12:28).

From this verse, we see that God can anoint you for other areas besides the fivefold ministry. He also anoints believers to be helps and administrators.

As a believer, it is critical to understand that the anointing is available to every child of God. That's why it is repeated several times in this book. If you are a child of God, you can receive God's anointing upon your life, not just the anointing within. When God's anointing is upon your life, you don't work hard for it. The anointing works for you. Therefore, anyone who has the anointing upon and understands how it works can demonstrate the power of God with ease.

It happens that way with me because I've got a special anointing upon my life that works all the time. I am very conscious of it. You can have the same power upon your life if you do exactly what God has written in His Word. You will receive that anointing and manifest it in your life all the time.

God has placed His Spirit in you and the anointing of God in your life can be increased. Once you reach that point where God's anointing increases, signs will follow you. You will cast out devils. You will speak with new tongues. If you drink any deadly thing, it will not hurt you. You will lay hands on the sick, and they will recover. You already have that anointing in you to cast out devils. Right now, you have the anointing of God in you to pray for the sick, and they will recover. You've got God's anointing in you right now, so if you eat or drink any deadly thing, it will not hurt you.

# Chapter 7

## The Benefits of the Anointing

People can fake charisma, but they cannot fake the power of God. The charismatic knows how to move the crowd. They are good orators and with their eloquent speech, they attract people. However, you can't fake the anointing. If you have the power, you have it. If you don't have it, you don't have it.

> And it shall come to pass in that day, that his burden shall be taken away from off thy shoulder, and his yoke from off thy neck, and the yoke shall be destroyed because of the anointing (Isaiah 10:27).

### Freedom

What did Isaiah mean when he said, "His burden shall be taken away from off thy shoulder and his yoke from off thy neck"? That means there will be no more weight. It is only the anointing of the Holy Ghost that can lift the burden and set us free. The power of God makes you feel light physically and spiritually. With the yoke off your shoulder, you walk free.

You don't just sing freedom. You live it at home, school, on the job, wherever you go.

The anointing of the Holy Ghost will take the yoke off your neck and destroy it. It is not good enough to simply remove the yoke because it may return. That's why the steps to freedom are twofold:

1. The yoke is removed
2. The yoke is destroyed

Every yoke of bondage in your life can be destroyed with the release of the anointing that breaks every yoke. Yokes of poverty in your life must go. Are you tired of being broke or sick?

*Every yoke of sickness and financial lack must go.*

> And it shall come to pass afterward, that I will pour out my spirit upon all flesh; and your sons and your daughters shall prophesy, your old men shall dream dreams, your young men shall see visions (Joel 2:28).

> The Spirit of the Lord God is upon me; because the Lord hath anointed me to preach good tidings unto the meek; he hath sent me to bind up the brokenhearted, to proclaim liberty to the captives, and the opening of the prison to them that are bound (Isaiah 61:1).

The anointing is the power of God; it is the overflow of the person of Jesus. It's the power of God working in you and through you. And when that power of God that is working in you is activated, nothing can keep you from moving forward.

## Healing

Once you carry that power of God upon your life, you walk in divine health. That's why I'm not sick, and I will never be sick. I have been saying this for over thirty years and you should too:

- I refuse to be sick!
- I will never be sick!
- The last time I was sick is the last time I will be sick!
- I will never be sick! In the name of Jesus.

## Refuse to be sick. Do not accept it!

I have a covenant with God that I will not be sick. You can tap into that covenant as well. As long as you are connected to God's mandate, the oil that flows in His house will flow in your life. You must believe it. Don't measure yourself against the lives of others. You don't know their beliefs. All pastors do not have faith. Many of them preach because they studied to preach. They went to school to learn how to preach. You don't need faith to preach. Why would you measure your life against that of a pastor who is constantly talking nonsense? If you have the call of God upon your life, God will take care of you. How can you preach when you are sick? God will make sure He protects you from every sickness. Declare that you will have no internal sicknesses because the anointing of God is working in you, in the name of Jesus.

The Bible says if that Spirit that raised Christ from the dead lives in you, it will energize, invigorate, and make alive your mortal bodies. Therefore, if the Enemy tries to send sickness to you, return it to the sender. Sickness does not belong in your body. You have too much work to do to be kept down. The reason some people get sick is because they accept it. You have a little pain in your finger and immediately, you say the pain is moving up to your shoulder; then it's going down to your knees. Make these declarations:

- I am anointed
- Anointed folks don't talk anyhow
- I refuse to kill myself
- I will remain healthy
- I will live healthy in the name of Jesus

As I said earlier, I have been saying these words for thirty years, so I know what I'm talking about. I'm not afraid to say them, and I will keep on saying them. I don't care what the Devil thinks. Don't use an example of somebody in Philadelphia who preaches every night and is sick as a reason for you to be sick. Next time, use my example. Don't make an excuse to be sick because somebody in California who is a bishop was sick for twenty years. Don't say, "But the Bible says Paul told Timothy use a little wine for your stomach ache." You are not Timothy. You have to understand how this thing works. You can't take something that is not good and claim it. The Word of God will work for you. What you believe in this Word will work for you.

If you read Scripture and focus on everyone in it who was depressed and begin to claim the person's life, you will also be depressed. Some prophets in the Bible were so downcast, they said, "God, just kill me." So if you're saying because that prophet was depressed, it's okay to be depressed, then you're going to get depressed. Was Jesus ever depressed? No. Are you sure? Was Jesus ever sick? Why? He is Jesus. You are too. You are Jesus.

I guess you are scared of that statement, but don't be. Jesus said, "I and the Father are one." Jesus also said, "You are one with Him." So what's the problem? I am Jesus and so, I am walking like Jesus. I am talking like Jesus. That's why I can heal the sick like Jesus. I can cast out devils like Jesus. I can call you to your destiny like Jesus. I can decree your promotion like Jesus. I can command money to come to your bank account like Jesus. Because I believe, I talk, I walk, and I live like Jesus.

The first advantage or benefit is walking in divine health and healing. In fact, the Bible tells us, let the inhabitants of Zion not say I am sick (Isaiah 33:24). I know many Christians have not read that, if they did, they would know good health is also for them.

## You Have Divine Revelation

> Olive oil for the light, spices for the anointing oil and for the fragrant incense (Exodus 25:6, NIV).

The anointing will change your life. This verse talks about oil bringing light, spices for anointing oil and sweet incense. The anointing oil brings divine revelation. It illuminates everything that is dark. It removes any kind of obscurity from your life. You will no longer walk in darkness because God's anointing upon your life brings revelation knowledge. Such knowledge enables you to move into the supernatural understanding of things in your life. God's anointing – both the one inside and the one that is about to come upon you in a different layer and dimension, brings divine, supernatural revelation.

## Provision

Once you have that anointing upon your life (remember I am saying "upon," not "in") you will never need anything.

There's constant provision. In 1 King 17:14, God's ability to provide every need is demonstrated. The widow of Zarephath was in a dire situation; she had no more food. In fact, all she had left for herself was her son, a handful of meal, and a small amount of oil.

> For thus saith the Lord God of Israel, The barrel
> of meal shall not waste, neither shall the cruse
> of oil fail, until the day *that* the Lord sendeth
> rain upon the earth (1 Kings 17:14).

This widow obeyed the instructions of the man of God and reaped the fruit of her actions. She had more than enough. That small portion of oil continued to bring provision. The oil represents the anointing. Once it comes upon you, everything about you changes. Once that anointing comes upon your life, you will never lack anything.

God told Elijah, "I have commanded that woman to feed you." God will provide. He has commanded. Actually, if He has to, God will even send a raven, the birds, to feed you. Do you know what the raven used to do for Elijah? The raven would go to the bakery, pick up a piece of bread, and bring it to Elijah every day.

The anointing brings an endless supply of resources into your life. God will supernaturally bless you. You will have continuous promotions and raises in your pay. Your business ventures will prosper. You will progress. Whatever you touch will succeed because the anointing is upon your life.

## Protection

Once you carry the anointing "upon" no stray bullet can locate you. The car that was headed in your direction to hit you will change course. You have divine protection and deliverance. If you ever get into a car accident it is because God wants to give you a new car and the insurance company must pay for it, not because you are at fault. God said, "Let Me just bless her with a new car. Let the person just hit her bumper so I can give her a new car." In fact, you will never die the death of another man because God will continue to protect you by the virtue of the Holy Ghost anointing.

> The Lord is my shepherd; I shall not want.
>
> He maketh me to lie down in green pastures; he leadeth me beside still waters.
>
> He restoreth my soul; he leadeth me in the paths of righteousness for his name's sake.
>
> Yea, though I walk through the valley of the shadow of death, I will fear no evil, for thou art with me; thy rod and thy staff they comfort me.
>
> Thou preparest a table before me in the presence of mine enemies: thou anointest my head with oil; my cup runneth over (Psalm 23:1–5).

## Blessings

> Behold, how good and how pleasant it is for brethren to dwell together in unity!
>
> It is like the precious ointment upon the head, that ran down upon the beard, even Aaron's beard: that went down to the skirts of his garments;

> As the dew of Hermon, and as the dew that descended upon the mountains of Zion: for there the Lord commanded the blessing, even life for evermore (Psalm 133:1–3).

The anointing does not flow upstream. It flows downstream. You cannot have what the head does not have. In other words, if the head is not anointed, nothing will trickle down to you. If the head is always complaining about poverty and disease, there is no way you and others under him will not complain. Consequently, whatever is released into your life will manifest in your life.

The head influences the rest of the body. If the head is struggling, inevitably, the body will struggle. You know the head contains the brain; if the brain is not working correctly, it affects the legs, hands, belly, toenails, eyes, and every part of your body. The head must function properly for the other members of the body to receive the benefits.

When you begin to get riches, don't stop going to church. Unfortunately, that's what many people do. They get little riches and think they have arrived. However, it is only the beginning. The blessings bring the riches. If you run with the riches, the riches might disappear. Stay under the blessing so the riches continue to flow endlessly.

## Power to Overcome the Enemy

The Enemy does not want you to know anything about the anointing because he was the anointed cherub, and he understands the working of the anointing. He knows what the anointing can do. He knows what the anointing can accomplish in the life of anyone. The anointing can make you succeed. The anointing can keep you on top. Without the anointing, I'm sunk. I'm in big trouble. God's anointing on and in my life gives me the confidence to stand boldly and declare the things I do because I know what God has put in me and what is upon me.

> But the anointing which ye have received of him abideth in you, and ye need not that any man teach you: but as the same anointing teacheth you of all things, and is truth, and is no lie, and even as it hath taught you, ye shall abide in him (1 John 2:27).

> But ye have an unction from the Holy One, and ye know all things (1 John 2:20).

But ye have an unction from the Holy one. That word "unction" in the above verse means the anointing. The anointing, which you have received from God abides in you. You have power in you.

> Ye are of God, little children, and have overcome them: because greater is he that is in you, than he that is in the world (1 John 4:4).

How do you feel having read that verse? How does it make you see yourself? It says you have already overcome them, not going to overcome them. You have already overcome the Enemy. Why? Greater is He that is in you. What scares you at night? Don't you know who you are? What makes you run around like a chicken with its head cut off? You have overcome them because the unction of the Holy Ghost is in you, the power of God resides in you.

Make these declarations:

- I have overcome them!
- Life cannot overcome me!
- Money cannot overcome me!
- Sickness cannot overcome me!
- Poverty cannot overcome me!

Never allow the Devil to intimidate you. Never! Never let those crazy, nonsense thoughts control your life. You control your thoughts because you are an overcomer. The next time the Devil brings thoughts in your mind, say, "Devil, sit down there. I am not going there. I am not thinking that one. I choose what I think. I am too much for that nonsense. I am too much for that thinking." That is the way you live the life of an overcomer.

Obviously, you believe the chair you are sitting in will hold you up? Why? Because the manufacturer said it can hold someone less than 300 pounds. And you believe you are less than 300 pounds. You have no fear it is going to collapse. You don't give any thought to sitting in the chair. You just do it. Yet, when God Almighty tells you something, you think about it. You try to figure it out. You are not sure. So you believe a manufacturer more than you believe God your Creator.

If every Christian would believe the Bible we would turn our world upside down. We will not allow employers to give us bad days. If an employer tells you, "You are fired" tell him, "Praise the Lord." If he tells you, "I don't like the way you do your job," say, "Hallelujah!" Yes. If he says, "Hey, Mr. Jeffrey, I have a yellow slip for you in the office" ask when you are supposed to resign and say thank you. Do you know when you do that your employer will be shocked? Don't cry about those things. You are too much for that.

*God is taking you somewhere.*

The unction was placed in your spirit the very day you were born again, the very moment you gave your life to Jesus, He placed an anointing in your spirit. He placed His power in your spirit.

# Chapter 8

## *Five Functions of the Anointing Within*

Electricity and the anointing have some similarities in the way they function. Electricity has certain laws when it flows. It produces light, heat, food, and air. Electricity does that in its normal state. The anointing within can be compared to electricity at room temperature or in a normal state.

Like electricity in its normal state, the anointing in its normal state is not always stable. It fluctuates depending on the resistance. For example, if I try to generate electricity by running wires from where I am all the way to the City Hall, it will lose its power as it goes the distance because of resistance. If I start with 500 million electrons, by the time I get to City Hall, it will probably have decreased to about 150 electrons. Similarly, resistance limits the flow of your power.

The anointing upon you operates by a different kind of law – the law of super conduction. That is when there is a consistent amount of current flowing from one point to the next. In other words, if it starts with 20,000 electrons at Point A, it will end with 20,000 electrons at Point B. The conditions will not affect the quantity, so if the temperature is raised or reduced the same amount of power will be generated.

The anointing upon you is very strong consistently. It's constantly powerful. On the other hand, the anointing within loses its intensity because of the resistance. You must understand the laws on which this anointing operates to flow effectively.

The power of electricity gets higher in cold temperatures or in wet places. There is a higher conductivity of electricity when the surface is wet compared to when the surface is dry because water conducts more electricity.

The anointing upon works through the theory of super conduction. Resistance is eliminated. It flows heavily. That's why I can lay hands on you and you feel as if electrical power has gone through you. Are you functioning at a capacity that is above and beyond the anointing within?

I will introduce two words. The first one is *exousia*, which refers to the anointing within. It is a delegation of authority and power. The delegation of authority is over serpents, diseases, demons, nature, animals, and the elements. The second aspect of exousia is power with God. This is different from the power of God. The power with God is as a result of your oneness, your *koinonia* (fellowship, communion) with the Spirit. When you fellowship with the Spirit, God's anointing within you, not only do you express the authority in that anointing but you have power with God because of your koinonia with the Spirit.

As mentioned earlier, the believer's anointing within comes as a result of the filling of the Holy Ghost. When I say filling, I mean exactly that; you are filled with the Holy Ghost and you begin to speak with other tongues. I believe from God's Word that speaking in other tongues is the entrance into the manifestation of the power of God upon your life. The

Bible says that as God's children, we have His anointing in us. If you are taught that everything you've always wanted is in your bedroom, would you search your kitchen? But if you were taught that what you need is in the kitchen you would spend all your life in the kitchen. Meanwhile, it has always been in your bedroom.

There are people waiting for the Holy Spirit to baptize them and they get frustrated because they don't see or feel Him coming on them. They cannot speak in tongues because they do not know that the Holy Ghost lives in them. The Bible says out of your belly shall flow rivers of living water.

If they only knew, they would not be looking for one filling to come on them. The priestly anointing comes as a result of the continuous filling of the Holy Ghost in your spirit. The Bible says, be filled with the Spirit. It is continuous filling with the Spirit because you cannot overflow unless you are filled up. Somebody once defined the anointing as the overflow of the person of Jesus, and they are right. But you cannot overflow if you are not filled to the top. You have to be filled to the top and keep on filling up to overflow. It is the overflow that brings about the manifestation.

> But ye shall receive power, after that the Holy Ghost is come upon you: and ye shall be witnesses unto me both in Jerusalem, and in all Judaea, and in Samaria, and unto the uttermost part of the earth (Acts1:8).

## Cast Out Devils

> And these signs shall follow them that believe; In my name shall they cast out devils; they shall speak with new tongues;

> They shall take up serpents; and if they drink
> any deadly thing, it shall not hurt them; they
> shall lay hands on the sick, and they shall re-
> cover (Mark 16:17–18).

When you study the Greek text, you'll realize this verse reads differently. The punctuation – commas, semicolons, and periods are not inspired. So when you read original manuscripts, you have a better understanding of what the scripture is saying. And once you understand it clearly, everything changes. Now, this is the way this verse should read, "And these signs shall follow them that believe in my name (put semicolon after 'in my name')." These signs shall follow them that believe in my name. Not just believe but "believe in my name." God delegates authority and power to those who believe in His name. When you restructure the sentence by shifting the punctuation marks, the entire meaning of the verse changes. It will read, "So these signs shall follow them that believe in my name. They shall cast out devils; they shall speak with new tongues; they shall take up serpents, and if they drink any poison it shall not hurt them. They shall lay hands on the sick and they shall recover." So the anointing "within" in the very first realm casts out devils. You have the exousia (power) over spirit beings that are devils.

It's very important that you tell demons they have no *exousia* over a human spirit. It's not the human spirit you should be casting out. That would be a devilish practice. God did not say, "In my name, you will cast out the spirit of John." He said you will cast out devils, not people.

So you have to be patient and love people. You don't cast away their spirits and let them die. If you are a Christian, and you are trying to kill everybody, it's not biblical. The Bible did not say kill your enemies. It said love your enemies and pray for those who persecute you. If they slap you on the right cheek, give them the left cheek. But if you cast out the Devil that is in them, they will stop slapping you. They will stop messing with you.

You have this authority that God has given to you over demonic spirits. As in the natural, so it is in the spiritual. Authority has to be released. If you have authority and you don't release it, it will not work for you. Every born-again child of God who understands this can cast out devils. So next time you see a devil, don't call your pastor. Tell yourself, "I got it. Devil, get out! In the name of Jesus" – because the pastor may be sleeping. You have to command that Devil to leave your home. You can't let him stay in your house for eight hours. If the Devil is manifesting in any of your children, you cast him out of those children. Don't wait until Sunday. No.

Most of us don't know we have power and delegated authority in Jesus' name; that's why we depend on the pastor for everything. You have the power in you.

Christians who know who they are, Christians who understand who they are in Christ, Christians who know they have exousia, do not need deliverance. Hey, I might have offended you but that's okay. Let it just sink in a little bit. Only those who don't know how the power works go around looking for prayer and deliverance. In fact, the Bible says you have been delivered from the kingdom of darkness and translated into the kingdom of God's dear Son. So which kingdom are you trying to be delivered from? The one you are in right now or the one you used to be in? How could you have been transferred, translated from the Enemy's kingdom into God's kingdom, yet, seek deliverance? From what are you seeking deliverance? Is it from light so you can go back to darkness? You are in the light, not in darkness. You have already been delivered from the kingdom of darkness and translated into the kingdom of light. You have the light of God in you. You have the light of God around you. There is no darkness around you. You walk in the light of God.

I want all Christians to get this in their spirits. I wish all Christians all over the world will get this in their spirits! You can walk in victory. You can talk victory. You can live victoriously when you put the Devil where he belongs. Don't say you want to be delivered. Delivered from what? Which devil? Where does that devil live?

You may say, "Pastor, be careful now; the Devil might come after you tonight." The Devil knows where I live. He can't even come close. He knows me by name. He knows me, and he knows you too. Don't run away from him. The Bible says the Devil roams around like a lion looking for whom he may devour. Notice, it says "for whom he may devour." That suggests he cannot devour everyone. You are not included in that "for whom" because the Devil cannot devour you. There's too much anointing in you for him to chew you. He will choke. God's anointing is already in you, and the Devil is under your feet. Don't give him credit. Don't give him any place in your life.

## Speak in New Tongue

You will speak in new tongues. What does that mean? God will give you supernatural communication with Him, a direct line to the almighty God. Praying in tongues is speaking directly to God. Can you pray in tongues? This is the gateway to experiencing the supernatural.

"They will speak in new tongues." Why will you speak in new tongues? Because there is a deposit of God's anointing within you. You have the Holy Spirit in you. There is no such thing as a second experience. We have been taught that we must try to be baptized in the Holy Ghost so we can speak in tongues. But that is not true. When you are filled with the Holy Ghost, you should speak in tongues. "They were filled with the Holy Ghost and began to speak in tongues" (Acts 2:4). It says, "The room they were in was filled with the Spirit" (Acts 2:4). "When they gathered in the upper room, that they were seated and the whole room was filled with the Spirit" (Acts 4:31).

Baptism is immersion. When you are baptized, you are dipped in water. You are baptized from your head to your toes. You are covered by water. Therefore, when you are baptized in the Spirit, your head to your toes are covered by the Spirit. The Bible says that the disciples were baptized by one spirit into the body of Christ. That is when they were born again. They were not born again when Jesus was with them. They were born again when they were baptized in the Holy Spirit. The infilling of the overflow of the Holy Spirit releases the heavenly language. That's why John 7:38 says, "Out of your belly shall flow rivers of living water."

If you are born again and you don't pray in tongues, you can do so. The anointing is already in you. Open your mouth and begin to speak it. That's it. It's as simple as that. The very moment you were born again, God gave you an unction of the Holy Spirit (1 John 2:20). Within that unction, there is a decoded language, tongues, which you can release from your spirit whenever you are ready. Every Christian can speak in the language of the Spirit.

The unction is a deposit of the Holy Ghost in your spirit. It is a decoded heavenly language to communicate with God's Spirit through your spirit. That's why the Bible says when you pray in tongues, your spirit prays. Your mind doesn't pray. Your spirit prays. It communicates with God directly. God will honor your prayer done in the spirit because your spirit man is communicating mysteries to God.

## Authority over Serpents

You will have authority over the animal world. Serpents are among the most dangerous or the worst of animals. The anointing within gives you power to command animals to sit, and they will sit. Perhaps, you already tell your dogs, "sit" and they do because you have authority over the animal kingdom.

## Authority over Natural Substances

If you drink any deadly poison, it will not harm you. You will be immune to poison. Whether you take it in through your mouth or veins, it will not kill you. If you are injected with poison, it will not kill you. I am not telling you to deliberately consume poison so you can check it out. That would be presumptuous. You don't put God to the test.

## Lay Hands on the Sick for Recovery

Sickness and diseases that suppress people's lives are the works of the Devil. Poverty is a work of the Devil. The Bible says you will lay your hands on the sick, and they will recover. Do you know that the Bible/God never specifically told us to pray for the sick? It only tells us, "if anyone is sick among you." In other words, being sick is not normal among Christians. Sickness should be foreign to the body of Christ. Therefore, if you have symptoms of sickness, don't call your friend claiming the sickness. You carry the anointing so you can lay hands on the sick and they shall recover.

Jesus Christ the Son of God came to destroy the works of the Devil (1 John 3:1–10). The Devil is a bad Devil. He is not good. Don't partner with him. Don't join his club. I made up my mind many years ago not to do anything that smells or looks like him or go anywhere that smells or looks like him.

Don't play with the Devil. Don't toy with Ouija boards. Don't call the psychic line. Don't expose yourself to the nonsense stuff of this world. Don't get yourself into witchcraft. Don't try to practice the things that God has forbidden. When the Devil gets hold of you, he will mess you up. He may promise you money and fame at the beginning. However, you can be certain he will take it all back and leave you broke. I repeat: the Devil is bad. That includes his in-laws and all his uncles. They are all bad. But God is a good God.

# Chapter 9

## How to Increase the Anointing Within

It is the plan of God that every one of us grows from glory to glory. We have established that we have God's anointing in us. But it's also important to know that the amount of the anointing we have in our lives can increase. Ezekiel talks about the water rising to the ankle level, then to the knee level. The water then rose above the knee level to the point where he had to swim (Ezekiel 47:3–5). Similarly, the anointing comes in different stages, and it can increase in your life.

God wants you to have the best, which only comes from Him. The anointing of God is a special heavenly commodity that God has given to every child of His. Hence, when you walk around, you can boldly tell everyone you see, "I'm anointed." They may be surprised if you tell them that, and they may not understand – but you carry the anointing in you. Given the significance and beauty of the anointing it is fair to say that you should desire more of it. But how can you increase the anointing?

> But the anointing which ye have received of
> him abideth in you, and ye need not that any
> man teach you: but as the same anointing
> teacheth you of all things, and is truth, and is
> no lie, and even as it hath taught you, ye shall
> abide in him (1 John 2:27).

In the above verse, we see that the anointing resides/abides in you and all born-again believers. When you continue to abide in the anointing of God, it manifests in your life. God's anointing is the power of God in you to do what He has destined you to do. It is the power of God to move in such a way you would not do normally.

## Intimacy

Understanding the anointing God has placed in you is the first step to increasing your anointing. The Spirit of God in you is full and without measure. The stronger God's power is in your life, the stronger you are. This anointing already has been rubbed in your spirit by the special grace of God.

Having an understanding of the Holy Spirit is not just talking about Him but having an intimate relationship with Him. It's about talking to Him like I'm talking to you right now. Once you get acquainted with the Holy Spirit, you are on the step of increasing that unction that He has put in you. It is the Spirit of God. It is the Holy Spirit that gives the anointing. He gives the enablement. He gives the inspiration. The very Spirit of God. The breath of God. The pneuma. The Holy Spirit is a person. He proceeds out of God, and He is God. You begin to look up to Him as your Father. And why do I say that? Jesus Christ Himself called Him His Father. And you can call Him your Father also. Jesus said, "My Father, which art in heaven." He also said, "My Father who liveth in me."

The more you respect the person of the Holy Spirit the more the anointing in you begins to increase, because He is the one who gives the power. When you are very close to Him, He talks to you. For example, I was in a situation where I asked Him, "What should I do right now?" He said, "Do this. Do that," and I obeyed. He said, "Step back," and I stepped back. The more you relate to Him, the more you talk to Him, the more you deal with Him, the more you know Him – the more of the anointing you will have. Make Him your best friend.

One day, I was about to pray for one man who could not walk. I was going to say, "In the name of Jesus, rise up and walk." The Holy Ghost said, "Stop. Ask him what he wants." I was shocked, and I stopped. I said, "What do you want?" He said, "I didn't come to stand up. I came to pray for my family members." Oh, my goodness. I would have wasted my time trying to command him to walk when that is not what he wanted in his life. He was in the wheelchair, and he was fine with it. What he wanted was for his family members to be saved.

If I had prayed, "In the name of Jesus rise up!" I would have been moved by my emotions, not the Spirit. I would not have gotten results. You must learn how to get very close to the Holy Spirit. Visualize Him as your blanket, your covering. He covers you.

The Holy Spirit's power in you becomes very vibrant. He begins to bubble. Have you ever sensed bubbling in your spirit? That is the power of the Holy Spirit. With more anointing, you will be amazed that you can do greater things than Jesus did.

The Holy Spirit of God that is in you wants to get acquainted with you on a higher level. I challenge you to talk to Him every day, not casually. Ask any questions and write down the answers. Ask Him simple questions. Ask Him which way you should go in the traffic? He will tell. Ask Him where there will be sales on certain kinds of food? He will tell you which store to go to. Ask Him who you should call or not call. He will tell you. When the phone rings, ask Him, "Holy Spirit, should I take the call or not? He will answer you. Because the more you get acquainted with Him, the more He knows you mean business. His power in you increases because now, He can trust you. They say power corrupts and absolute power corrupts absolutely. Therefore, God wants to trust you before He gives you increased power. He doesn't want to give you increased power for you to misuse or abuse.

## Get the Word of God into Your Spirit

The number two way to increase that anointing that is in you, is found in Numbers 11: 4–8,

> And the mixt multitude that was among them fell a lusting: and the children of Israel also wept again, and said, Who shall give us flesh to eat?
>
> We remember the fish, which we did eat in Egypt freely; the cucumbers, and the melons, and the leeks, and the onions, and the garlick:
>
> But now our soul is dried away: there is nothing at all, beside this manna, before our eyes.
>
> And the manna was as coriander seed, and the colour thereof as the colour of bdellium.
>
> And the people went about, and gathered it, and ground it in mills, or beat it in a mortar, and baked it in pans, and made cakes of it:

and the taste of it was as the taste of fresh oil (Numbers 11:4–8).

The Bible says the Old Testament is a shadow of the things to come. The manna the Israelites received was the seed. In the Bible, the seed often refers to the Word of God. Jesus gave us the Parable of the Sower. He said if you don't understand this parable, you cannot understand anything in the Word of God because the Word of God is the seed. If you don't understand that the Word of God is a seed, then nothing works in your life. Here, we can see that the Bible says the manna was a seed.

After all the beating and grinding of the manna, it tasted like fresh oil. Fresh oil speaks of the anointing of God upon our lives. When you eat the Word of God, meditate, grind, and study, you will siphon the anointing from that Word. And that anointing will begin to manifest in your life. What am I talking about? I am saying that you need to study the Word because if you want God's power to increase in your life, that's where the power of God is found. You cannot have increased anointing without knowing the Bible.

As you travel around Africa and even here in America occasionally, the gas in your car may run out, but there may be no gas station nearby. You call your friend, and he shows up. You park your car next to his, and you put a tube in the car. You begin to siphon (with your mouth) the gas/petrol from your friend's car to your car. As you draw and taste a little of the oil, you put the tube in the car and the oil is transferred to the empty car. The Word of God, which is the bread of life, the food, the oil, operates in like manner. The more you siphon, the more you receive.

I remember years ago, I probably had over ten to fifteen Bibles. Thank God for the computer. Back then, there were no iPads. So I would spread out about 15 Bibles, and I would check one verse in all the different translations. Sometimes, I would probably stay awake until five in the morning because I wanted to chew the Word. I would read, check references, and use the concordance to make sure I got it right. Thank God for the concordance. It took a lot of time, but I would search and dig into the Word. No wonder the anointing is strong in my life.

## Prayer

The third way to increase the anointing is by prayer. Some people don't know how to pray. Some people don't even try to pray and some sleep while praying. Somehow, you are not sleepy when you are engaging in other activities but when it's time to pray, your eyes get heavy. Somewhere between "Father, in the name of Jesus..." and "Amen," nothing was said; you were sleeping.

Anytime you are praying and you find yourself getting sleepy, get up, walk around, and continue to pray. The Enemy knows the more you pray, the more you are tapping into the Rock because it is the Rock that releases the oil – the anointing of God.

Don't think the anointing of God will start flowing in your life if you don't pray, read your Bible or love the Holy Spirit. Don't expect you will have a greater release by simply singing in church on Sunday morning, "Fresh anointing fall on me. Fresh Holy Spirit come and take control." Take which control? He has not even controlled your morning hours. You just get up, brush your teeth, take your shower, eat, and go to work. You never have enough time to say, "Holy Spirit, good morning."

I never talk to anybody in the morning without telling the Holy Spirit, "Good morning" first. Even if my wife greets me in the morning and I have not spoken to the Holy Spirit, I do not answer. I just keep quiet. Let me talk to the Holy Spirit first. You see, without Him, there would be no her. He comes first. Some people try to please their spouses before God and mess up their lives. When you please God, He will take care of your spouse.

## Watch Your Association

Last but not least, if you want to increase the anointing in your spirit, watch your associations:

> There is treasure to be desired and oil in the dwelling of the wise; but a foolish man spendeth it up (Proverbs 21:20).

Those with whom you associate can increase or decrease the anointing in your life. If you go to the wrong place of fellowship, the anointing will dry up. If you're going to a place where the anointing of God is not flowing, where the people are dried up and they are dead, the little anointing you have will be extinguished. The Bible teaches, "There is treasure to be desired and oil in the dwelling of the wise; but a foolish man spendeth it up." This refers to your associations and how they will determine the increase or the level of anointing in your life. Who are your friends? Who do you spend your time with? Who do you chitchat with? Are they Christians? Do they believe in the anointing? Are they moving in the anointing? "Deep calleth unto deep" (Psalm 42:7).

The anointing of your friend or those close to you rubs off. You can't help it. It just happens. It's the law that God has put in the universe. On the other hand, just like bad communication corrupts good manners, evil associations will hinder the anointing. If your friend is a criminal, sooner or later God help you, you will become like him. If you are traveling in your car with your friend who is a drug dealer or drug addict, and you are pulled over by the police, you may be in big trouble. What happens if they find drugs in your friend's pockets or in your car? You may be sent to jail. By what? Association.

Be in the place where God's power is moving. Associate with people who believe what you believe in. Spend time with those who are anointed. The anointing you respect and honor is the one you will attract in your life. The anointing you despise will never work for you.

# Chapter 10

## How to Release the Anointing Within

God has called apostles, prophets, evangelists, pastors and teachers to equip the church. God's anointing lives in you. It is the very power of God in you for a reason.

But ye have an unction from the Holy One, and ye know all things" (1 John 2:20).

But the anointing which ye have received of him abideth in you, and ye need not that any man teach you: but as the same anointing teacheth you of all things, and is truth, and is no lie, and even as it hath taught you, ye shall abide in him (1 John 2:27).

Now unto him that is able to do exceeding abundantly above all that we ask or think, according to the power that worketh in us (Ephesians 3:20).

Some pastors have jobs – to be pastors. On the other hand, some pastors are men of God. They speak for God. Whatever they declare under the anointing comes to pass. That's because they release the anointing within.

Jesus was anointed, so He had the authority to kick out the money exchangers. He released His anointing in that situation. If somebody else had done the same, it would not have had the same effect.

The anointing within will not work unless it is released. You can have all the power within your spirit. If it is not released, it will not work. You will go to your grave with the anointing within. The anointing upon can be released by contact or by presence. However, the anointing within is released in a different format or in a different way.

When Jesus was on earth, He revealed to us, that the power of the Spirit lives within and the power of the anointing upon.

> It is the spirit that quickeneth; the flesh prof-
> iteth nothing: the words that I speak unto you,
> they are spirit, and they are life (John 6:63).

The anointing within or the believers' anointing depends on the words that we speak. In as much as this may sound simple, you must take it very seriously if you want the anointing within to work for you. Whenever you release the believers' anointing, it is through spoken words. However, the anointing upon is released by contact without saying a word. I can release the anointing upon a towel or cloth, and you can take that cloth to someone who is bedridden for that person to be healed. I don't have to say a word, only make contact. Scripture supports this:

So that from his body were brought unto the sick handkerchiefs or aprons, and the diseases departed from them, and the evil spirits went out of them (Acts 19:12).

The handkerchiefs that came into contact with Paul's body were taken to the sick for them to be healed. The handkerchiefs traveled everywhere, but they still retained the power. That is a demonstration of the anointing upon, but the anointing within doesn't work like that. The anointing within is released by speaking. Words are powerful. Yet, many believers use them incorrectly. Words are to be used to take authority

You cannot be as dumb as Adam. Adam was so dumb, the Devil was talking to his wife, while he stood there saying nothing. At that time, God had already given him dominion over everything on earth. He could have told the serpent, "Get out of our sight! Go there and sit down." Instead, he said nothing. He remained quiet and allowed the Devil to wreak havoc in his life. Don't sit quietly by and let the Devil mess up your family. Don't let him make your children sick. Declare: "I will not be quiet anymore!"

My daughter was at death's door. Actually, the doctor said she was gone. With the anointing upon me, I simply remained calm. But her mother got very violent in the spirit and said, "In the name of Jesus, this child must live and not die. I come against you Devil." As a matter of fact, she was screaming so loudly, the nurses ran back into the room. But that anointing within was released and in a couple of minutes later my daughter's eyes were open. You have to open your mouth when you are faced with life's difficult situations.

In another instance, there was heavy lightning. I sensed in the spirit the lightning was about to hit my house. But I didn't tell anybody. I simply prayed in the spirit and commanded that lightning to go in a different direction. The Devil was trying a nonsense trick. But I didn't sit there quietly. I said, "In the name of Jesus, I command that lightning to divert." I declared the Word. If you just sit there and say, "Oh my God. The flu is coming now, you're going to get the flu because you spoke it into existence. Instead, say, "No. In the name of Jesus, flu doesn't belong to this body."

But that is not enough. You may say but you have been saying that all along, but to no avail. The sickness is still there. Nothing is changing because the anointing within has another factor. Mark 16:17 says, "And these signs shall follow them that believe." Those who believe in the name of Jesus exercise faith. If you don't believe in His name, these signs shall not follow you. Your faith level controls the amount of believer's anointing that is released in your spirit. It is the faith level behind the spoken word that releases the anointing Within.

> For verily I say unto you, That whosoever shall say unto this mountain, Be thou removed, and be thou cast into the sea; and shall not doubt in his heart, but shall believe that those things which he saith shall come to pass; he shall have whatsoever he saith (Mark 11:23).

"He who believes what he says." Do you believe what you say? Note carefully, it's believing what you say, the words you have spoken, not what you feel inside that causes a thing to come to pass. Releasing the anointing within is believing what you say. Do you believe in what you say or do you just believe in what you believe? You have believed all these years in what you believe without realizing that believing in what you say is what releases that anointing within.

Sad to say, many Christians don't believe in what they say. That's why they talk in any manner. It is what you say the most that you truly believe in. What have you been talking when nobody is near? You can believe you have the anointing in you; it's working in you. But what are you saying? Keep your mouth shut if you have nothing meaningful to say. Don't talk to everybody either. You cannot pray, "Oh, God, give me a job. God, give me a job. I believe I got it." Then the next moment you tell your friend, "I have been applying for a job for the last six months. Nobody called me for interview." It's the last statement you made that you believe because if you believed the former, you would have stuck with it.

## Do not change your confession.

If you change your word, it is because you have no faith in what you said. If you have faith in what you say, you will not change your confession.

If you doubt your words, the anointing within will not work. You may have to keep repeating the Word to encourage your faith. The Bible says faith comes by hearing and hearing by the Word of God. Build your faith. Don't wait until you see the evidence. The anointing within does not depend on evidence. Simply believe what you said would happen and that's it. Control your words when you speak concerning any circumstance. Do it in faith. Again, the anointing within is released through words spoken in faith.

At Spirit Temple Bible Church, God has blessed us greatly. We have such a wonderful time in His presence. His power is demonstrated and the favor of God is unleashed upon our lives. We experience His favor beyond measure – uncommon favor. We have the uncommon favor of God upon our lives and ministry and the Devil can do nothing about it. He can be upset and mad but that is his problem.

This cosmos is full of power. Don't go through life without power because power is available. Be strengthened in the

Lord. Carry the power of God in your life so the Enemy doesn't make you his prey. He's looking for those he can destroy. Who is he looking at? Who is he searching for? Those people who don't have the power of God in them to repel him? The power of God in your life shields you from the Devil. He is blinded when he looks in your direction because you carry so much power. The Devil is afraid of you. Inevitably, he will attack you, but it will not work. His efforts will be wasted and futile. The power of God will strengthen you to walk victoriously, not just talking it but living it – experiencing victory in every area of your life.

One of my mandates is to bring people into God's presence and to release God's power in the lives of others. God doesn't want you walking around on this earth being used, abused or misused by the Enemy. You are a child of God. You carry God's power in you. God's anointing upon your life makes a big difference.

As explained earlier, the anointing upon you is like a superconductor. The power is so strong that the Enemy is literally afraid of you. Do you want the Devil to run from you? There's a price to pay. Once you pay this price, you receive the dunamis power of God.

# Chapter 11

## Preparation for the Anointing

Elisha wanted to receive the mantle, the double portion of Elijah's anointing on his life but he had to go through four places to reach that level. He had to pay the price by going through Gilgal, Bethel, Jericho, and Jordan.

You can pray until heaven comes down if you don't go through Gilgal, pass through Bethel, experience Jericho, and cross over Jordan, you will not receive the mantle. It won't happen. Have you gone through Gilgal? Have you gone through Bethel? How about Jericho? Have you crossed over Jordan?

> And it came to pass, when the Lord would take up Elijah into heaven by a whirlwind, that Elijah went with Elisha from Gilgal.
>
> And Elijah said unto Elisha, Tarry here, I pray thee; for the Lord hath sent me to Bethel. And Elisha said unto him, As the Lord liveth, and as thy soul liveth, I will not leave thee. So they went down to Bethel.

And the sons of the prophets that were at Bethel came forth to Elisha, and said unto him, Knowest thou that the Lord will take away thy master from thy head today? And he said, Yea, I know it; hold ye your peace.

And Elijah said unto him, Elisha, tarry here, I pray thee; for the Lord hath sent me to Jericho. And he said, As the Lord liveth, and as thy soul liveth, I will not leave thee. So they came to Jericho.

And the sons of the prophets that were at Jericho came to Elisha, and said unto him, Knowest thou that the Lord will take away thy master from thy head today? And he answered, Yea, I know it; hold ye your peace.

And Elijah said unto him, Tarry, I pray thee, here; for the Lord hath sent me to Jordan. And he said, As the Lord liveth, and as thy soul liveth, I will not leave thee. And they two went on.

And fifty men of the sons of the prophets went, and stood to view afar off: and they two stood by Jordan.

And Elijah took his mantle, and wrapped it together, and smote the waters, and they were divided hither and thither, so that they two went over on dry ground.

And it came to pass, when they were gone over, that Elijah said unto Elisha, Ask what I shall do for thee, before I be taken away from thee. And Elisha said, I pray thee, let a double portion of thy spirit be upon me.

And he said, Thou hast asked a hard thing: nevertheless, if thou see me when I am taken from thee, it shall be so unto thee; but if not, it shall not be so.

And it came to pass, as they still went on, and talked, that, behold, there appeared a chariot of fire, and horses of fire, and parted them both asunder; and Elijah went up by a whirlwind into heaven.

And Elisha saw it, and he cried, My father, my father, the chariot of Israel, and the horsemen thereof. And he saw him no more: and he took hold of his own clothes, and rent them in two pieces.

He took up also the mantle of Elijah that fell from him, and went back, and stood by the bank of Jordan.

And he took the mantle of Elijah that fell from him, and smote the waters, and said, Where is the Lord God of Elijah? and when he also had smitten the waters, they parted hither and thither: and Elisha went over (2 Kings 2:1–14).

## The Gilgal Level – Cutting off Fleshly Desires

At Gilgal, you cut off your fleshly desires. You let go of all those things that you always wanted to do, your rights, and sinful pleasures. You release them all because it's part of the price you have to pay for God to entrust you with His precious commodity – the anointing. Gilgal represents overcoming the world, conquering your flesh, dying to yourself, and dying to the flesh. That is, you do not allow the flesh to rule you anymore. Sad to say, too many Christians let their flesh control them. The flesh makes them get mad and upset. They can't move past that place. But if you are to move to a higher level of the anointing you must die to self. If you have difficulty dying to self, pray about it every day, "God, I want to die to self. Please. I want to die." Pray earnestly and be assured that if you are still in Gilgal, there is hope.

Gilgal is a place where you surrender everything, where you are crucified with Christ. It's no longer you who live but Christ who lives in you. Consequently, the things that used to bother you in the past do not bother you anymore. Anger is no longer in your vocabulary. You don't walk around like a time bomb that's waiting to explode. That's Gilgal. God wants you to overcome all of that.

I die a thousand times every day. No matter what anybody does to me, I'm dead. You need to die too. If somebody curses you, you're dead. If somebody calls you a bad name, say, "The Lord is good." You see, the Enemy is trying to take you back to Gilgal. He wants you to remain at the fleshly level. He desires to stunt your progress. If you're still in Gilgal, it's difficult to have the anointing of God upon your life. That's why there are very few men and women who carry the anointing. Most of them are not willing to pay the price. They want to remain at the point where they fight for their rights. "It's my right. I have the right to be angry. I have the right to be mad." If you want to reach Gilgal, you have to give up those rights and make up your mind to let God control your life completely.

I love the story of the Prodigal Son who left his father's house with his portion of wealth. He faced all kinds of problems in his life. He even ate from the pig pen. Does the Bible say somebody prayed for him? No. It doesn't say that. What it does say is that he came to himself. He said, "I have made up my mind. I am going back to my father." You must make up your mind not to let the flesh control you. Understand you have a part to play in receiving God's anointing upon your life. The office God puts you in, is His choice. But God's anointing and the levels of power upon your life are your prerogative. They are not determined by God. You decide how far you want to go with Him.

No longer will you allow anything to make you fall into temptation. You can't keep saying the Devil made you do it. "The Devil made me get mad. The Devil made me sleep around." Which devil? The Devil is not that strong. Have you ever seen the Devil? Have you ever seen the Devil entered your house? Have you eaten with him? Have you seen the Devil took off your shoes? Has he untied your shoelace? Have you seen him made you decide? Did he put on your clothes? Did he help you brush your teeth or your hair? No, let's be real. You made up your mind. You chose. So don't give the Devil that power. You decide to die daily. See, when you die to your flesh, you activate something real in your life. You activate your spirit man.

Until you overcome these fleshly desires, God cannot entrust you with His power. Ask God to help you. He gives you the ability to overcome, but you have to be willing and obedient to do what He says. I believe with all of my heart that God has called everyone into the ministry of reconciliation. To succeed in that ministry, you need the power of God. I believe every Christian is a minister. Everybody has been called into ministry. So ministry is not just done from the pulpit. There are other aspects.

Ministry is much more exciting when you are doing it with the anointing of the Holy Spirit, when you know that God is backing you up. It's important to know your employer is supporting you. You don't have to worry about anything. He empowers you. God who has anointed you will back you up. However, to get the anointing, you must first of all die to the flesh. You must be willing to go through Gilgal.

You must continue on this roadmap to experience a higher level of God's anointing. There's always more. God is inexhaustible. You cannot exhaust or frustrate Him. There is so much about God you cannot fathom with your natural mind. The power of God is so great that the things He can do in and through your life cannot be explained. He wants to do mighty works through you. However, He is waiting for you to pay the price. Everything has a price tag, including the clothes you wear. Even your salvation has a price tag. It's not cheap. Jesus paid for it.

The first time we read of Gilgal is in the book of Joshua.

> And the Lord said unto Joshua, This day have I
> rolled away the reproach of Egypt from off you.
> Wherefore the name of the place is called Gilgal
> unto this day (Joshua 5:9).

Gilgal was where the Israelites who departed from Egypt were circumcised. Those who were in Egypt got circumcised before the exodus. However, many were born after, and it was in Gilgal that their circumcision took place. It was the renewal of a covenant that God had made with Abraham to circumcise, to roll away the foreskin. At Gilgal, we roll away anything that impedes us from being all God wants us to be. Gilgal represents circumcision, a cutting away.

> In whom also ye are circumcised with the cir-
> cumcision made without hands, in putting off
> the body of the sins of the flesh by the circum-
> cision of Christ (Colossians 2:11).

If you desire to be anointed by God, you cannot be like anybody else. They can go to the movies, but you can't. Your eyes cannot behold and find pleasure in iniquity. So if you want to see the supernatural, but you focus on junk, you will be defeated. It will not work. Light and darkness cannot coexist. Do you want to hear God speak to you? Do you want to hear His voice? If so, you cannot give your ears to evil. I emphasize once again, Gilgal is a place of death. It is a place where those around you know you are dead. The flesh doesn't communicate with God. The flesh doesn't talk to God. The flesh is an enemy of God.

Man was made in the image of God. He has God's likeness but was corrupted by Satan. But man is still able to create. Even the man who is not born again can create. The man who doesn't go to church can still create because God made us like Him.

One time, mankind was trying to build a tower to reach heaven. If God had let them, they would have done it. Human beings can do whatever they put their minds to do. Most people who fail in life are those who refuse to try. God will never give up on you. The only person God will give up on is the person who gives up on himself. As long as you refuse to give up on yourself, God will always be there. The moment you give up on you, what can God work with?

Those men who were building the Tower of Babel worked with one mind, one goal, and one purpose. With such unity and determination, they could have achieved anything. But God literally confused their language so they could not communicate with each other. Men and women can achieve great things, even though they are not Christians. How much more the children of God with the power of the anointing? You have unlimited possibilities if you just tap into that power. Non-Christians are willing to pay the price to achieve their goals. Unfortunately, many Christians don't overcome because of laziness. We are too lazy to pray and even attend church. If you sincerely want to overcome the flesh and go through Gilgal you can, but you have to make up your mind and press forward.

> That which is born of the flesh is flesh; and that which is born of the Spirit is spirit (John 3:6).

> And he said to them all, If any man will come after me, let him deny himself, and take up his cross daily, and follow me (Luke 9:23).

Did the Bible say take up your cross once a week? Did it say once a year? Is it on Sunday and then you leave? No, the Bible says we must take up our cross every day. By the way, taking up your cross doesn't mean carrying it on your chest. The cross represents death.

> I protest by your rejoicing which I have in Christ Jesus our Lord, I die daily (1 Corinthians 15:31).

The voice of your flesh is your feeling. You are guided by your emotions. You don't feel like doing this. You feel like this. You feel like that. At Gilgal, you can no longer listen to the voice of the flesh but the voice of the soul. The voice of the soul is reasoning. Of course, the voice of the soul is much better than the voice of the flesh. But the voice of the soul can still mislead you. Then there is the voice of the spirit, which is your conscience. If your spirit has been recreated, you have a high success level in your life because you are led by the spirit, not by your flesh or your soul.

> Do not love the world or anything in the world.
> If anyone loves the world, love for the Father is
> not in them (1 John 2:15, NIV).

Jesus overcame Gilgal when He was in the wilderness through the life of fasting (Luke 4:2–14).

Gilgal is a place of dying to self. It's a place of circumcision. It's a place of death. It's a place of fasting. Fasting kills the flesh more than anything else. A constant life of prayer and fasting is vital on your roadmap to higher levels and preparation for the anointing.

Every Christian is a candidate to be used by God. However, if you want God to really use you, you really have to be dead. When you deal with the flesh through fasting, it takes you to the place called Bethel.

## The Bethel Level

The next stop on the roadmap to a higher level of the anointing is Bethel. Bethel means the house of God, a place of communion, a place of worship. It is a place where you grow in your relationship with God, a place where you desire the presence of God more than anything else, a place where God's presence means everything to you, a place where you just can't wait for the church doors to open. You've got to get to that place where nobody has to remind you to go to church. It's a place you get to where you long to experience God again. You are so eager to be in His presence. God becomes real in your life, and His presence is tangible. You must get to Bethel? How? By developing a right relationship with God and being in His presence. The power of God is found in the presence of God.

> And Jacob went out from Beersheba, and went toward Haran.
>
> And he lighted upon a certain place, and tarried there all night, because the sun was set; and he took of the stones of that place, and put them for his pillows, and laid down in that place to sleep.
>
> And he dreamed, and behold a ladder set up on the earth, and the top of it reached to heaven: and behold the angels of God ascending and descending on it.
>
> And, behold, the Lord stood above it, and said, I am the Lord God of Abraham thy father, and the God of Isaac: the land whereon thou liest, to thee will I give it, and to thy seed;
>
> And thy seed shall be as the dust of the earth, and thou shalt spread abroad to the west, and to the east, and to the north, and to the south: and in thee and in thy seed shall all the families of the earth be blessed.
>
> And, behold, I am with thee, and will keep thee in all places whither thou goest, and will bring thee again into this land; for I will not leave

thee, until I have done that which I have spoken to thee of.

And Jacob awaked out of his sleep, and he said, Surely the Lord is in this place; and I knew it not.

And he was afraid, and said, How dreadful is this place! this is none other but the house of God, and this is the gate of heaven.

And Jacob rose up early in the morning, and took the stone that he had put for his pillows, and set it up for a pillar, and poured oil upon the top of it.

And he called the name of that place Bethel: but the name of that city was called Luz at the first.

And Jacob vowed a vow, saying, If God will be with me, and will keep me in this way that I go, and will give me bread to eat, and raiment to put on,

So that I come again to my father's house in peace; then shall the Lord be my God:

And this stone, which I have set for a pillar, shall be God's house: and of all that thou shalt give me I will surely give the tenth unto thee (Genesis 28:10–22).

Above is the story of Jacob in the place he called Bethel,

the place where God is. In his dream, we see the angels going back and forth from heaven. The Bible makes it very, very clear that God was with Jacob in that place. Bethel is a place like no other. It is different from Gilgal. At Bethel, there is a highway or the high gate to heaven giving direct access to God. What does that have to do with the anointing? Bethel speaks about dwelling in God and standing in His presence, which is vital in your quest for the anointing.

After you have gone through Gilgal, the next step is to be in a place where you and God can commune in a time of prayer and fellowship. A place when nothing else matters in your life but God. God will not put His precious commodity on your life if you don't treasure His presence. In His presence, there is power. The power of God is the anointing of the Holy Spirit. Jacob and God communed at Bethel.

This was the secret of Elijah. He knew the presence of God and that without it, there is no real anointing. You've got to seek God and desire to be in His presence. His presence must be more important to you than food! It must be more important to you than your friends, husband, wife, and children! You must desire God's presence more than Facebook, Instagram or any other social media platform.

## God's presence must come first place in your life!

Elijah often announced his ministry by saying, "I am Elijah who stand in the presence of God." He always said that. No wonder this man of God used his mantle to just smack the water, divide the river into two, and walk on dry land.

> And Elijah said, As the LORD of hosts liveth, before whom I stand, surely, were it not that I regard the presence of Jehoshaphat the king

of Judah, I would not look toward thee, nor see thee (2 Kings 3:14).

Here, you can see Elijah referring to the presence of God because that is where he always stood. He was always in God's presence.

And Elijah said again as the LORD of hosts liveth, before whom I stand, I will surely show myself unto him today (1 King 18:15).

And Elijah the Tishbite, who was the inhabitant of Gilead, said unto Ahab, As the Lord, God of Israel, liveth before whom I stand, there shall not be dew nor rain these years but according him to my word (1 King 17:1).

Elijah said, "according to his word." Why? He was always in God's presence. He and God understood each other. He continued: "There shall be no dew or rain these years but according to His word." Elijah was able to perform great miracles because he remained in the presence of God. He could call things into being because of his intimate relationship with God. He understood that the power of God is in the presence of God.

One thing I discovered about God is that He knows your heart. He knows what you're thinking. You can't hide from Him. If you go to the East, He's there. If you go to the West, He's there. If you hide in your closet, God is there. He knows your heart. You cannot fool Him on Sunday morning by singing, "How great, your presence is Heaven to me." You can't simply get emotional for thirty minutes, go home, and blast devilish music in your house all week. You can't watch pornography and evil movies filled with immorality and expect to be in the presence of God. These things only feed the flesh. They are God's enemies and will not invite His presence in your life, home, or church. To remain in His presence, you have to give up some friendships, bad habits, and things you like to do. Give up Facebook if you have to. If Facebook is always in your face and you are not seeking God's face, you cannot be in His presence.

Get on your knees. Ask God to speak to you. Pray continuously until you get the answer. Hence, when you say, "Thus says the Lord," it's not from your head but from the Lord. Your head can mislead you. As a leader, I seek God earnestly. I remain in His presence until I hear His voice because I don't want to mislead anyone. Ask God to build your desire to get past the outer court and go into the inner court where there is the Holy of Holies. God's presence will bring increase, and it will improve your life for the better. Things will happen miraculously. You don't have to be stressed about anything – where you have to stay, what to eat, finances or anything else. God will take care of you.

Elisha was determined to go all the way. He didn't stop in Gilgal. He knew what he wanted and he went after it. Elijah told Elisha, "Stay back; don't come." Elisha said, "Nope. I am coming with you. Wherever you go, I am going. I need to experience the same anointing that is upon your life even double in the literal sense of it." He was willing to pay the price. When his master told him to wait for him, perhaps, he was testing to see if he was really serious. To receive God's anointing upon your life, you have to be serious. When I say serious, I don't mean to wear a frown on your face or look angry. Rather, I am saying you have to be highly determined.

God has a plan for every one of us, and He has more on the horizon for you. You can experience more of His glory, His grace – manifold grace and uncommon grace. Jesus Christ already paid the price for us to receive salvation. However, if you want to receive God's anointing or to increase it upon your life, you have to go through this road map – Gilgal, Bethel, Jericho, and Jordan.

Just being nice to your neighbor will not get you the anointing. Attending church every Sunday is just part of it, but that alone will not bring the anointing on your life either. What matters is the time you spend in your secret place with God. It's your relationship with God and what you discuss when no one is there. It's the power you receive in His presence – at Bethel.

## The Level of Jericho

At Jericho you learn that you have authority over the demonic realm and the powers of the Enemy. Jericho speaks about our victory over the Enemy and His works. It is about the walk of faith because to defeat the Enemy, you need to have faith. You cannot operate by feelings. You need faith because the people you call your enemies are not your enemies. Your real enemies are demons and demonic forces that control the lives of people.

Jericho talks about faith. It represents when you trust God with your heart. To receive God's power on your life, you must understand how faith works. We know that faith comes by hearing and hearing the Word of God. Therefore, you must build up your spirit man with the Word of God to facilitate the growth of your faith. That way, you can do what God has called you to do. Remember, faith is the legal entrance into the realm of the supernatural. Therefore, without faith you cannot operate in the supernatural realm.

On the day after the Passover, on that very
day, they ate some of the produce of the land,
unleavened cakes and parched grain.

The manna ceased on the day after they had
eaten some of the produce of the land, so that
the sons of Israel no longer had manna, but they
ate some of the yield of the land of Canaan during
that year.

Now it came about when Joshua was by Jericho,
that he lifted up his eyes and looked, and behold, a man was standing opposite him with his
sword drawn in his hand, and Joshua went to
him and said to him, "Are you for us or for our
adversaries? (Joshua 5:11–13, NASB).

In the plain of Jericho, manna ceased. It no longer fell
from heaven. The Israelites had to eat of the fruit of the land
of Canaan. Joshua was in Jericho and there, a man stood
with a sword in his hand. Joshua asked him, "Are you coming
to support us or to support the adversary?" You see, the
Israelites had to cross Jericho to get to Jordan. They had
three options:

1.  Go through Jericho and deal with the challenges ahead
2.  Stay and mingle with those in Jericho
3.  Go back to the place they left

Jericho is the lowest place on the earth. It's about 1,300
feet below sea level. Joshua met this man, a man of battle,
definitely the Lord, as you can see. It was there that the man
who stood before Joshua answered, "No. I am not for you. I
am not for them. But as captain of the host of the Lord I am

now come." Joshua fell on his face and he worshipped and said, "What message do you have for me from the Lord?" In essence, the man was saying, "I am here to take over. I'm not here to be on the side of the adversary. I'm not here to be on your side either, but I'm here to take over."

No longer did the Israelites have to wait for God to give them manna in the morning. They would have to live by faith for their provisions. When you get to Jericho, you live by faith. Without faith, you cannot experience the anointing and without the anointing, the glory of God will not manifest. The glory of God is seen when God does things irrespective of what man does or thinks. Man has to step aside and let God operate for His glory. It's when God touches peoples' lives without anyone laying hands on them. It is when God does what He's doing on His own: healing, comforting, and just taking care of His children His way.

At Jericho, the Israelites had to live by faith. They had to trust God that whatever was planted would bring food. They could no longer just fold their hands and say, "In the morning when we wake up there will be food right there." No. God was teaching them a lesson of trust and complete reliance on Him. He made the point that before you get to the Promise Land, you must learn to trust Him.

God will not give you His anointing if you are full of fear. You've got to believe everything He says in His Word and that settles it. You cannot be moved by what you see. Only be moved by what God's Word says. For God to release His power on your life, He needs to know that you have gone through your own Jericho; that you are not walking by sight or by numbers but beyond what you see in the natural.

> Now Jericho was straitly shut up because of the children of Israel: none went out, and none came in.

And the Lord said unto Joshua, See, I have given into thine hand Jericho, and the king thereof, and the mighty men of valour.

And ye shall compass the city, all ye men of war, and go round about the city once. Thus shalt thou do six days.

And seven priests shall bear before the ark seven trumpets of rams' horns: and the seventh day ye shall compass the city seven times, and the priests shall blow with the trumpets.

And it shall come to pass, that when they make a long blast with the ram's horn, and when ye hear the sound of the trumpet, all the people shall shout with a great shout; and the wall of the city shall fall down flat, and the people shall ascend up every man straight before him.

And Joshua the son of Nun called the priests, and said unto them, Take up the ark of the covenant, and let seven priests bear seven trumpets of rams' horns before the ark of the Lord (Joshua 6:1–6).

Jericho was shut up. It was completely locked up because of the Israelites. No one went out and no one came in. And the Lord said unto Joshua, "See that I have given unto you Jericho." Isn't that something? The Israelites had not even entered Jericho yet. Nevertheless, God said, "I have already given it to you." Therefore, it took faith on the part of Joshua to believe what God said. Joshua could have said, "But God, I don't see it yet." God says, "I have given you the money." You respond, "But God, I don't see it yet. God, I want to see the manifestation." God says, "I've given you already." You say, "Oh God, no, I have not seen my results yet." God says, "But I've given you." You say, "Oh God, no, I've not seen the husband yet. Until he puts a ring on my finger, I will not believe it." You doubt God. However, what did Joshua do? He obeyed God's instructions to march around Jericho for six days and on the seventh day walked around seven times. After that, Joshua was told to blow the trumpet after which the walls of Jericho would collapse.

To overcome the Enemy in your life, you must live by faith. Remember, the Israelites walked around the city of Jericho six times. Six represents the number of the effort of man. Seven represents the number of God, completion. It was when they went around Jericho seven times on the seventh day that they let go of self. God stepped in because they trusted Him until the end. Some of the people must have complained in their hearts. Others must have doubted. What God said may have seemed silly and illogical, but Joshua believed by faith and reaped the rewards. Like Joshua, God wants us to keep going through Jericho by faith.

You must start trusting what God says. If you never trusted God before, start trusting Him now. Even if your life is going down south, still trust Him. Believe me, God can lift you up and take you from down below. Only God can call light out of darkness. God can change your life in an instant.

Walking in faith is not only about performing mighty deeds and miracles. You don't have to wait for the big things. Have faith that your children will go to school and come back home safely. Have faith that you will not die of hunger. Have faith that you will not be homeless. Have faith that you will not be thrown on the roadside.

Even when you have faith and you are evicted, have faith

that God has a better plan for you. That's how it works. Never change your confession. Even if you have faith that you will never lose your job but you are fired the next day, you should be praising God and shouting Hallelujah! God has something in store for you.

If you believe God you say, "God, I still praise You. God, I thank You. It doesn't matter what I see. I refuse to see what it is. I'm looking beyond what I see." Don't be fazed by those who will talk about you, castigate you, lie on you, and try to frame you. Don't quit. Tell yourself they can gather but they will scatter. No weapon formed against you shall prosper. Any tongue that rises against you in judgment is condemned in the Name of Jesus. You have faith in God.

Be strong in the Lord and the power of His might. Put on the whole armor of God. Walk like a lion. Walk like a champion because that is who you are.

## The Level of Jordan

Finally, we go to Jordan. What exactly does Jordan represent? What exactly does Jordan mean? Jordan represents overcoming the soul life within you. It is subjugating your soul to the things of the spirit. Crossing over from the soulish realm to the realm of the spirit. In other words, bringing your soul under the control of the spirit.

The soul is a connector between the physical realm and realm of the spirit. I want you to pay close attention because this will help you see yourself moving forward with God's power in your life. Your soul is the gateway to your spirit. The connection between your body and your spirit is the soul. Hence, if your soul has not been taught how to be subjugated to the spirit man or to the Spirit of God, God's power cannot come upon your life because the anointing is spiritual. It's not physical. It is tangible, yet, spiritual. The power of God is here right now as I write these words. I feel power in my body. However, it's not originating from my body. So how can I feel it in my body? There is a transmission from the spirit to the soul to the body. If my soul is not in line with the spirit, my body will not experience the power. It is a matter of learning how to allow your soul to be submitted to the spirit to live on earth. To live on earth you need a human body, and so, you must learn how to go from the natural to the spiritual life. God wants us to be in the spirit all the time, but if we are always in the spirit, what would happen? You can not live on this planet. Therefore, the soul helps you transfer from the spirit to the natural. The soul is the go-between.

You see, we live in two worlds. I am here. I am also there. Right now, if I choose, I can instantly enter the spirit realm. And I can instantly return to the flesh (the natural world) by choice. The point is that understanding how to subjugate your soul to your spirit man is a gateway to receiving the power of God upon your life.

> And Elijah took his mantle, and wrapped it to-gether, and smote the waters, and they were divided hither and thither, so that they two went over on dry ground.
>
> And it came to pass, when they were gone over, that Elijah said unto Elisha, Ask what I shall do for thee, before I be taken away from thee. And Elisha said, I pray thee, let a double portion of thy spirit be upon me.
>
> And he said, Thou hast asked a hard thing: nevertheless, if thou see me when I am taken from thee, it shall be so unto thee; but if not, it shall not be so.

> And it came to pass, as they still went on, and talked, that, behold, there appeared a chariot of fire, and horses of fire, and parted them both asunder; and Elijah went up by a whirlwind into heaven.
>
> And Elisha saw it, and he cried, My father, my father, the chariot of Israel, and the horsemen thereof. And he saw him no more: and he took hold of his own clothes, and rent them in two pieces.
>
> He took up also the mantle of Elijah that fell from him, and went back, and stood by the bank of Jordan;
>
> And he took the mantle of Elijah that fell from him, and smote the waters, and said, Where is the Lord God of Elijah? and when he also had smitten the waters, they parted hither and thither: and Elisha went over (2 Kings 2:8–14).

The level of Jordan is a significant milestone to reach in your Christian journey. It was after crossing the River Jordan that Elijah asked Elisha what he wanted. Elisha desperately desired a double portion of the spirit of Elijah. Elijah told him he had to see his departure to receive it. I can imagine Elisha never blinking his eyes. I doubt he even slept because he wanted to make sure he was constantly on the alert. He didn't want to miss the opportunity to get the double portion of the spirit. Not long after that, Elijah was taken up to heaven. He received the mantle, and he did exactly what Elijah did. He struck that water again and walked on dry land.

The "double portion" Elisha requested does not mean

twice the amount. Rather, it refers to seniority as the chief prophet. It does not mean if Elijah performed seven miracles that Elisha would do fourteen. The double portion means that he had double of what everybody else had or he is a senior in the family. In that culture, the oldest child always received double. If you had seven children, they would divide the inheritance into eight portions and the older child got two portions. Everybody else got one each. That signified that the eldest was the one representing the family. It does not suggest the acquisition of double what your source has.

When I use the word "double" portion in reference to the anointing with Elisha and Elijah, I'm not referring to numbers. It's possible that he could have gotten double of what Elijah had but that is not what double portion refers to in this particular context. Elisha became the senior prophet so when other prophets saw him, they knew he was carrying the mantle Elijah once had. He could not hide it.

The Israelite's crossing of the Red Sea represents water baptism. Crossing the Jordan River represents going into the spiritual realm God desires for us. God doesn't want you to remain in Gilgal or Bethel. He doesn't want you to just stay in Jericho. Reaching those stages are great accomplishments, but He has more in store for you. He wants you to cross over Jordan. He wants you to be acquainted with the spirit world. You cannot receive His power in your life if you don't understand how the spirit world operates. If you're constantly filled with the things of the natural world, you will never truly receive God's power in your life. Crossing Jordan subjugates your soul. Your soul represents emotions, your thinking, and your will. So you have to bring your will, emotions, and thinking under the control of the Spirit of God.

You cannot receive God's full power if you are still living in Gilgal, Bethel or Jericho. Jordan, where the Spirit of God controls you is the place for the double portion. Many of us understand that God has made us spirit, soul, and body. However, we also need to realize that He really wants us to live in the Spirit. Like I said earlier, your spirit man communicates with your body through your soul. Your soul is very important. But if it is not submitted to the things of the Spirit, you can forget about the anointing. It will not work.

When Elisha and Elijah struck the River Jordan, what happened? It divided and became dry land. They walked through dry land. That was a decision that was made. That represented a decision you have to make to subjugate your thinking, your soul, your emotions to the things of the Spirit. The things of the Spirit should be what you think about at all times. Crossing Jordan represents getting away from your constant thoughts, emotional reminiscences and the natural circumstances.

> Having the understanding darkened, being alienated from the life of God through the ignorance that is in them, because of the blindness of their heart (Ephesians 4:18).

All the time, your soul is being influenced to choose the spirit or the natural realm. Crossing over Jordan means you've crossed over the influence of the natural realm and now your soul is consumed with the things of the Spirit. Your thinking is controlled by the things of the Spirit.

Ephesians 4:18, refers to the unregenerated soul – minds, wills, and emotions that have not been reformed by Christ. Your understanding is darkened because you are ignorant of the things of God. And because your heart is blind, you cannot see. All you think about are the things of this world. But to receive God's power upon your life, you must get away from that mindset and go into the realm of the Spirit.

For they that are after the flesh do mind the things of the flesh; but they that are after the Spirit the things of the Spirit.

For to be carnally minded is death; but to be spiritually minded is life and peace.

Because the carnal mind is enmity against God: for it is not subject to the law of God, neither indeed can be.

So then they that are in the flesh cannot please God (Romans 8:5–8).

Do you want to receive God's anointing? On a scale of one to ten, how much do you think about the anointing of God?

Every day for weeks and months, I said, "God, I need this. I know I've gone through Gilgal. I've gone through Bethel. I've gone through Jericho, and now, I've crossed over to the River Jordan. Now, God, I focus my mind. Everything I listen to has to do with the Spirit of God." Not long after that, God moved mightily in my life. And it has never been the same since that day. I remember that day. I recall where I was when it happened. When God's power hits you, it's not by accident. You will just know it because something tangible enters your life and you are never the same again.

You cannot watch too much TV anymore. You can't spend all day on Facebook, Twitter, and Instagram. Are you willing to give them up? God is saying, "I want your time, now." Will you say, "Oh God, please, this soap opera, it always makes me laugh." Do you depend on the soap opera to give you joy and happiness instead of the Holy Spirit? You may say, "I gotta pay some money to go to this comedy show." And every weekend you're in a comedy show. Why? Because you want to laugh. So you want to tune into a comedy show hosted by somebody who doesn't even know Jesus, who castigates the Holy Spirit so you can laugh. Your laughter will probably last as long as the show. And that's it. The Holy Spirit doesn't like that.

The point is you need to just give up many things in your life, at least, anything that competes with God. Give it up! I know it is difficult for some of us. But how hungry are you for the Spirit of God? If you're really hungry, you'll do it. If you really desire God's power in your life, you will do whatever it takes. You'll give up TV. You will have to give up going out every week and watching those shows that eat into Bible study time and prayer. Too many Christians miss Bible study because they don't want to miss their favorite TV shows.

"Sometimes, instead of seeking the face of God, you seek the face of your friends. You check to see what people are wearing, what's new, what is the status of a friend. You want to see what everyone else is doing. You spend three, four, five hours on social media then you say, "Oh, thank you Lord Jesus. Jesus, you know I love you so much. Thank you, Lord Jesus." You take a shower and say, "Jesus, you are so faithful." You come out of the bathroom quickly, and head straight for your next round of Facebook. So Facebook gets more time than Jesus. You cannot fool God. He knows where your priorities lie. He knows you're not serious.

You only want to pray when you're about to fall asleep. You barely get to say, "Lord, now I go to bed, keep my family. Amen." But when your phone rings, you can't wait to grab it. You talk for three, four hours. If you sincerely want to cross over Jordan, you need to subjugate your soul, thinking, and emotions to the Spirit of God. Your spirit man will not function if your soul does not cooperate. Let me just make this very clear. Your spirit needs your soul to operate.

Do you understand? If your soul is not in cooperation with your spirit, no matter how the anointing wants to flow, it will not flow. Why, because your soul is still hooked on what it saw last evening on Facebook. What your mind is preoccupied with is what manifests in your life. If your mind, your soul is preoccupied with God's power, you will experience more of His power in your life. You become what you see. It will take you further away from your destiny or bring you closer to your destiny. Everything you see affects you. Everything you hear affects you. Everything you think about affects you one way or the other. Why do you think companies pay millions of dollars for a thirty second commercial? So you can see what they have to offer. You are drawn to buy their products. Some of you will get into your car and drive for miles to get something you saw in an ad on TV. You gravitate more to what comes into your face.

If we speak about the anointing of God all the time, we gravitate more towards the anointing of the Holy Spirit. If we think about sickness all the time, any little pain in your side you will think is cancer because in your mind, sickness prevails. If we talk about demons and the Devil every day – the Devil in your bedroom, the Devil in the AC, the Devil in the flower, the Devil in the church, the Devil everywhere – do you know you will be so conscious of the Devil that everything you see will have the Devil in it? However, when you talk about God, He will be constantly in your life and mind. God is in your house. God is in your car. God is in your spirit. You will see God in everything around you.

> I beseech you therefore, brethren, by the mercies of God, that ye present your bodies a living sacrifice, holy, acceptable unto God, which is your reasonable service.

> And be not conformed to this world: but be ye
> transformed by the renewing of your mind, that
> ye may prove what is that good, and accept-
> able, and perfect, will of God (Romans 12:1–2).

Renewing your mind is a process. Subjugating your soul
to the Spirit of God is an instant decision. Are you following
me? You have to renew your mind with the Word of God
daily, gradually. But choosing not to think on the things of
the Enemy is an instant decision. Crossing over Jordan is
immediate.

> And it shall come to pass, as soon as the soles
> of the feet of the priests that bear the ark of
> the Lord, the Lord of all the earth, shall rest in
> the waters of Jordan, that the waters of Jordan
> shall be cut off from the waters that come
> down from above; and they shall stand upon
> an heap (Joshua 3:13).

The moment their feet touched the water, the water dried
up. The water is symbolic of the fact that the entrance of your
soul into the spiritual realm is a decision you have to make.
You decide to focus your mind and thinking on the face of
the Spirit.

You may not always understand why you're doing something, but you have to do what the Spirit says. God will
give you understanding after you have done what He asks.
Sometimes, we do many things because we understand what
we are doing. Other times, we do things even if we don't
understand. Allow yourself to do what God says even if you
don't quite understand.

## Important Points to Remember

1. Go through Gilgal. Die to self. Let go of those self-desires: the things that you want to do that God says don't do or the plans you have that are contrary to the plan of God. Gilgal represents a place of fasting.
2. Have a desire for the Spirit and the presence of God.
3. Walk by faith all the time and not by sight. God's anointing requires the walk of faith. Many times, you may not see with your physical eyes what God is doing in the realm of the Spirit. So you have to walk by faith.
4. You must subjugate your soul, mind, will, and emotions to the things of the Spirit. When you do that, and you wait on God, and the right timing, God will put His power upon your life. You will forever be grateful that you did what you had to do to receive the power of God.

As said before, and worth repeating, the anointing is the overflow of the presence of Christ. The anointing is the power of God. The anointing is the overflow of the person of Christ. The anointing brings about a change, not only in your life but around you and anything that comes into contact with you.

My desire, dream, goal, and mandate on this earth, in this season, is to bring about the teaching or the ministry of God's anointing. Let us welcome God's presence in this entire region. We need to bring His presence back to the church and our lives so His anointing flows through us. When you have God's presence in your life, you have God's anointing. God's anointing is the power of God. When the anointing comes on you, the power of God controls you. The power of God moves you.

The power of God repels every fly. Flies represent the Devil. Flies represent evil. In the Old Testament, the shepherds would anoint the sheep with oil and the flies would not touch them. When God's anointing is upon you, the devils literally takeoff.

When they try to come close to you, they are repelled. Every child of God has been destined to receive God's anointing. Every child of God has a covenant right to receive God's anointing, to have God's power, not only in you but on you.

In the second dimension of the anointing, you can see angels. You can see into the spiritual realm. You can see what is of God and what is not of God. Everything you see is not necessarily from the Holy Ghost. It is the anointing within that gives you the witness that what you see is from the Lord. Sometimes, the Enemy will disguise situations to make you think God is showing you something when it is all his doing. However, the anointing within will let you know you are protected and the Devil cannot touch you. Learn to develop the anointing within.

If what you see on the outside does not line up with the inside, you must discard it. That is why the anointing within is priceless. It's the very first dimension and every child of God has it. But not every child of God knows how to develop that anointing within. Until you know how to develop the anointing within, the anointing upon cannot get manifested in the dimension God wants it to be in. God gives the anointing at different levels and stages within the second dimension. You may start off with a little quart of anointing on your head.

The Bible says the anointing upon Aaron dripped from his head all the way down. The more you wait upon God, the more you trust Him. The more you pray, the more you desire God. The more you let the anointing control you, the more it grows. And even with that, God still puts a limitation on the anointing upon you. Everyone does not have the same level of anointing upon them. There is still a limitation, so you would not step into territories that God has not called you into.

> But ye shall receive power after the Holy Ghost
> is come upon you (Acts 1:8).

Have you received the Holy Spirit with evidence of speaking in tongues? It's very important for every child of God to do so. Why? Number one, the Devil has no clue what you are talking about. The Devil does not know where you're going or where you're coming from. Words are spirit, and when you start speaking words in English, guess what? The Devil understands English. He understands Spanish, too. Stop posting your status on Facebook. Don't tell the Devil your next move. The Bible says the children of the world are even wiser than Christians. Don't tell your enemy where you're going to be in the next thirty minutes. How about if he sets a trap for you there?

It's better when you surprise the Devil. Be unpredictable when it comes to the realm of the spirit. Don't let him know which way you're moving. The Devil may dig a pit for you where they think you are going, but because the spirit changes your course, your enemies will fall into that same pit.

To speak in tongues, you must get away from your head. You don't have to know everything that you are saying. Let the Holy Ghost speak through you. The Lord told me when I got home one day that the reason He needs some people to sleep, so He can perform surgery on them. God cannot work on some of us when we are awake. When you are self-centered and self-absorbed, God can't work on you. Therefore, He said, "Be still and know I am God." So when you are still and out of this physical realm, God moves in your life. Many times when you are sleeping, God can work on you because you are not in this flesh.

I grew up in a place where the man of God who was a leader and mentor to me in the early stages of my born-again experience would pray for me. I would go home and in the night as I slept, God would work on me through dreams. I have heard many testimonies from people who received healing and revelation through dreams as they slept. For example, someone would say, "Oh, my God. I went to bed last night and when I woke up my belly that was swollen was down. I saw somebody performing surgery on my belly and all the pain is gone." Learn to be still. Speaking in an unknown tongue gets you out of your mind. You have to depend on the Holy Ghost to speak through you.

> The Spirit of the Lord is on me, because he has anointed me to proclaim good news to the poor. He has sent me to proclaim freedom for the prisoners and recovery of sight for the blind to set the oppressed free (Luke 4:18, NIV).

The Spirit of God was literally upon Jesus. The anointing of the Holy Ghost was on Him. The Spirit of God comes upon you, so you can preach the gospel effectively. Jesus said He was sent to heal the broken-hearted, to preach deliverance to the captive, recovery of sight to the blind, and to set at liberty them that are bruised and hurting. God's anointing upon you causes you to act like Jesus Christ.

I know what I'm saying because growing up, I belonged to a particular church. Someone I thought was a friend wanted to hurt me, and to see if I still had power within me.

I had just returned from Saudi Arabia, and I saw this young man who was my schoolmate in elementary school. I was overwhelmed with compassion to help him so he could excel in life. I wanted to help him succeed, but I did not know his plans were evil.

He came to my brother's house, and I was sitting on a chair in a corridor facing the door. He was sitting facing me on the opposite side. He told me, "Please, I need to get some water." Suddenly, God opened my eyes, and I saw a snake moving in his belly, literally. The Lord told me, "Nope. Don't get up." I told my brother's wife, "Please, get me some water for my friend." My friend went, "No, no, no. I want you to get me the water."

And I said, "No, bring the water for him."

He said, "No, I want you to get up and get the water."

She brought the water for him to drink. I said, "Drink it," but he staunchly refused.

I insisted vehemently, "Drink it now!"

Let me tell you, when God's anointing comes upon your life, there's a level of boldness that comes upon you. I forced the water down his throat. And when he drank the water, whatever was moving in his belly just settled down.

He asked me, "Do you still go to that church?"

I said, "Of course. Just because I went overseas doesn't mean I'm not faithful to God's calling on my life." I said, "What were you trying to do? You have to tell me what your plan was." Do you know what his plan was? He was going to spit the venom on me when I got up for the water.

What am I saying here? I'm saying to you right now that you need the anointing upon you. If you don't have God's power on you, you are vulnerable; you will be messed up. The power of the Holy Ghost is the absolute power you need upon your life.

I'm a very shy person. As a child, I didn't even like to talk because I stuttered. I couldn't pronounce words so I kept quiet most of the time. I would sit in my little corner and just be quiet. I would never ask a question in class and only spoke when called on. That's the kind of young boy I was. But when the anointing comes upon you, suddenly, you can speak. You are not afraid of anybody or anything. By nature, I was cool. I mind my business and didn't get stressed out about life. But when God's anointing came upon me, I am ready to go into any territory and take back what the Enemy has stolen.

# Chapter 12

## Levels and Dimensions of the Anointing

The word "anointing" was first used by the shepherds in relation to their sheep. To get rid of the parasites and ticks that cling to the bodies of some sheep, the shepherds would anoint the sheep with oil. Parasites are there to suck the life out of the sheep but when the oil is applied the ticks fall off. The word "anoint" means to rub on, to smear with oil. So the shepherds anointed the sheep with oil to stop the parasites from creating friction on the sheep. And sometimes, they also applied the oil to the sheep continuously to keep the parasites, the ticks, and the bugs away.

We are sheep, and we have a Shepherd. Who is our Shepherd? Jesus. As a pastor, I am an under-shepherd. It is a major responsibility for a man of God to take care of the sheep. The under shepherd is expected to apply the oil on the sheep to free them from the onslaughts of the parasites. The number one mission is to keep the ticks away. The number two mission is to remove the ticks from your body.

The parasites or the ticks represent demons, the Devil, and everything they bring along with them. So the function of that oil, even for you as a child of God, is to keep the

Devil from sticking to you or from affecting your life. You may have heard the term, "sheep without blemish." A sheep without blemish is one that has a constant application of oil every day in preparation for a special service. Sheep without blemish were used as sacrifices to God. He wanted them for service. Such sheep went through a process from the day they were born. The shepherd applied oil to the sheep and prepared them for a special time of sacrifice, for a special purpose. Hallelujah!

As God's people, when we talk about the anointing of God, we are identifying it as a rubbing of God's power on our lives. As a consequence, demons cannot stick to you. Sickness cannot stick to you. Poverty cannot stick to you. Diseases cannot stick to you; they just fall off. That's why the Bible says, "The yoke is broken by the reason of anointing." The yoke is like a chain holding you in bondage. However, once you are anointed, it has to let go. It just breaks off. That's what the anointing is supposed to do. Having a clear understanding of the anointing and its purpose helps you tremendously as a child of God. God has a distinct plan and purpose. He wants to give every one of His children the oil and to rub a special anointing on them so every Devil and tick will leave them alone.

Bear in mind though that the first anointing cannot be the only one. Do you know the ticks return to attach themselves to the sheep? Each time they come back, the shepherd applies the oil. He has to anoint them with oil again.

## The First Level of the Anointing

At the first level, although you have God's anointing on you, it is still possible for demons to oppress you. You have the anointing all right, but ticks attach to you and suck your blood. Have you met people who are anointed but have problems?

Demons still beat them up at night. They can't sleep. They're still struggling with demons of sickness, poverty, lack, and all kind of problems. They have sleepless nights, but they are anointed. They are God's anointed; they are Christians. Do you know the story of King Saul, in the Bible? Was King Saul anointed? Yes. Did he have demons? Yes.

Indeed, He was anointed, but demons attached to him. Demons messed with him. If you are at level one in your Christian walk, you will experience a similar situation. God has not taken His anointing off your life because you're His child. But the demons are still there. You can't sleep, and it feels as if when you touch something, it breaks. The anointing brings life to whatever you touch.

King Saul had the demon of jealousy. That's why he relentlessly tried to kill David. Some pastors also have demons of jealousy; yet, they are anointed.

Sometimes, David had to play music to drive away the demons that tormented King Saul. One day, while King Saul was pursuing David to kill him, David found King Saul asleep with his sword. David had the perfect opportunity to destroy his enemy, Saul. Yet, as much as he wanted to kill Saul, he didn't. God said, "Touch not my anointed, or do my prophet no harm."

I remember as a teenager in Nigeria, we went to a Christian camp where we stayed in dorms. We called it "retreat" back then. A young Christian who was very vibrant for the Lord was being oppressed by demons every time he went to bed at night. He would scream, "Leave me alone! Leave me alone!" The boy was a Christian who was anointed, but those demons were still affecting him. One night, I said, "Let us switch beds." I was thinking perhaps, the demons would not know which bed he was in. So I slept on his bed. Despite our exchange, the same demon oppressed him. So the demons pretty much knew where he was.

It reminds me of my little niece who was a Christian for many years. Yet, the demons were attacking her. She couldn't sleep, and they would tell her to kill herself sometimes. Even though her parents are Christians, the demonic spirit was attached to her. However, one day, I prayed for her over the phone, and she was completely delivered. The demons left her, and she came back to her senses. She is perfectly whole now.

As Christians at level one, demonic spirits still affect our finances, relationships, health, and other areas of our lives. You praise God, but they're still there. I pray that, today, you will determine in your heart to move from level one and be free in the name of Jesus.

## Level Two Anointing

The level two anointing has no power. You pray for other people; they get better. You pray for yourself; nothing happens. All the people you pray for get well, but you, if you have a simple pain in your toe and you pray, the pain remains. Somebody may have a heavy tumor in the stomach. You pray for the person and that tumor disappears. However, you can't seem to get healing for yourself. You are anointed but the power doesn't work for you. You can't even pray to get rid of an ordinary headache. In fact, when you pray, it gets worse. If somebody else has a headache and you pray, it leaves. Your level of anointing must change. You need the level two anointing.

It is like Barabbas and Jesus. Many of us really don't understand too much of the story of Barabbas because we have been taught the same thing all along so we never really studied Barabbas. Many of us thought Barabbas was a bad criminal. No. He was a leader. Barabbas was anointed. His name was Jesus Barabbas. Pontius Pilate thought if he said Jesus Barabbas, the people would ask to release Jesus Christ, but they didn't.

The name "Barabbas" basically means Simon Bar-Jonah, which is Simon the son of Johnna. There was Jesus the Son of the Father and Jesus Barabbas, the son of the father. While Jesus is the Son of God, Barabbas was the son of the father. Barabbas was anointed but had no power. So when the priest said, "Let's choose. Should I release Barabbas, the son of the father or Jesus, the Son of God?" he thought they would say, "Give us the Son of God." However, they said, "No. Give us the son of the father." Again, Barabbas was anointed without power. Jesus, the Son of God had all power.

So you have people who are anointed but carry no power. They pray for others and lead others, but they can't help themselves. They prophesy to others, but never receive a prophecy for themselves. It seems as if God gives them words for other people, never for themselves. How come God is talking to you about a sister, but He never talks to you about you?

God gave me a word for me. I prophesied that word, and I recorded it. I am saying this to let you know that God can talk to you through you. Don't just ask God to give you a word for another sister. No, ask God to give you a word for you. And He will. He will talk to you for you.

In the past, people often called me from nowhere asking, "Please apostle, please can you give me a word? What is the Lord telling you about me?" I would tell them to ask their pastor that question. In fact, some came saying, "Please, pray for me; pray for me." I would say, "Have you told your pastor yet?"

Their response would be, "He has no power; he doesn't

pray." Then why are you there? He doesn't pray for you, but you go there every Sunday.

You say "Hey, I'm just there because I love the pastor." But he can't pray for you. The pastor himself is sick; he can't even pray for himself. He's broke. How can a broke person lift up another broke person? No. You must know how this thing works. The anointing does not flow upstream; it flows downstream. If the head is not anointed you cannot get up there. You can't.

## Level Three Anointing

The third level of the anointing is anointing with power. It is where no obstacle can stop you from succeeding. You have the unlimited power of God. You've gone past the level of anointing where you are oppressed by demons or the anointing where you help others but you cannot help yourself. Now, you are in a place where you have God's power, not only to help others but for you. You can actually manifest God's power everywhere, anytime. It's working for others and also working for your life.

That is God's plan for every one of His children. You don't want to be anointed, yet, you are faced with demonic spirits attacking your family, your life, and messing with you. No. We want you to be anointed and put the Devil to run. We saw the example of Jesus Christ. He was anointed with power and even death could not hold Him back.

Even when sickness tries to come, the anointing on you stops it. The sickness cannot stick because the anointing upon your life just washes off everything that tries to come against you. The Bible says they will gather, but they will scatter. They will plan, but they will not succeed. Many have planned against you, but did not succeed. People plan against ministries, but they don't succeed. You can't plan against the house of God and think you will win.

When your enemies try to attack you, they will never succeed and that is why the Bible says, "No weapon formed against me shall prosper." They will try to form it, but it will not prosper because you carry God's anointing – the level three anointing, which is anointing with power.

## The Well Dimension of the Anointing

God gives you a well anointing that quenches your thirst. It is inside you and empowers you to handle situations in your life. The well anointing will satisfy your spiritual and emotional needs. You don't need a car, house, or any material things to be happy. You simply need the well level of the anointing in your life.

> Jesus answered and said unto her, Whosoever drinketh of this water shall thirst again:
>
> But whosoever drinketh of the water that I shall give him shall never thirst; but the water that I shall give him shall be in him a well of water springing up into everlasting life (John 4:13–14).
>
> But the anointing which ye have received of him abideth in you, and ye need not that any man teach you: but as the same anointing teacheth you of all things, and is truth, and is no lie, and even as it hath taught you, ye shall abide in him (1 John 2:27).

This anointing guides, leads, and teaches you all things. It tells you where to invest your money. It tells you how much seed to sow. It tells you which friends not to have, who you should not marry and who to marry. It tells you things you must do, and what you must not do. It tells you, "Go to Spirit Temple Bible Church."

You must keep on drinking from the well of God to keep this particular anointing moving on your behalf. The problem is that many Christians are ignorant of this well dimension. They do not know that they carry it.

> My people are destroyed for lack of knowledge: because thou hast rejected knowledge, I will also reject thee, that thou shalt be no priest to me: seeing thou hast forgotten the law of thy God, I will also forget thy children (Hosea 4:6).

The people of God were led astray because of their ignorance. They refused to seek knowledge. Don't reject the anointing because you lack knowledge. You will lose as a result. This anointing has to be stimulated so it can bubble on the inside. This well anointing, this level, this dimension of God's anointing makes things manifest in your life because every word you speak comes from the inside.

In heaven, every word spoken is a material object. When you say door, a door shows up. When you say car, a car shows up. When you say money, money shows up. When you say blessing, a blessing shows up. But you must understand that you have this dimension. Every child of God carries this dimension. You operate in this dimension and lack nothing if you understand that you have it. You don't have to beg God for anything because you have God in you. You just speak it out of that consciousness.

## *Live life from the inside.*

If you can just get this, you will change your world. If you stop living from the outside, if you stop making decisions based on what you see, you will achieve exceedingly above what you can ask or think. Don't live from the soulish or physical realm. If you do, you will limit yourself. I know it's a challenge but please, start somewhere. Don't say what you feel or what you hear from the external voices. Speak what emanates from the spirit man. Because every word spoken from the inside manifests in the natural realm.

Some of us received no inheritance so all the things many of us have today originated from our innermost beings and were produced on the outside. I pray that our children will apply this principle to their lives and not depend on what is left for them. But the Bible says that the righteous man leaves an inheritance for his children's children. So before you settle to leave a car for your son, think about your great-grandson. So don't think, "My son will just live in my house." What about your great-grandsons. Where will they live? It's that parochial mentality that limits your capability. You think you're small. Think bigger. The Bible says, leave an inheritance for your children's children. "

You can do it but you have to start believing instead of thinking, "I'm barely making it. I'm living in the land of Barely Making It Boulevard." No way! It does not matter if you are barely making it now. Don't say you are barely making it be-cause once you say you are barely making it, you are living based on the external factors. Your spirit man is rich; it's blessed; it's prosperous; it's wealthy; it's healthy. It's rich with wisdom.

The well anointing safeguards you from false prophets, false apostles, false teachers, false pastors, false brethren who want to lead you astray or lead you into captivity. That's important but God doesn't want you to stop there. We sing a song sometimes, "From the inside, from the inside of me, Cause all I want is for you to be glorified. So let healing rise from the inside. Let joy rise from the inside. Let prosperity rise from the inside. Set me on fire from the inside." It has a profound message: from the inside.

Then why are you not doing it? Why is everything coming from the outside? "I don't feel right. I don't like the way you talked to me last night. You looked at me the wrong way. You didn't hug me right." That is living on the outside. Imagine if everybody lived on the inside. There'd be so much peace and love, as well as less stress. If you live from the outside, you will be stressed all the time. I've gotten so used to living from the inside that people might think I am insensitive. No, I just don't live on the outside. I am not there. I don't live in that place. I can't live like that, so I live on the inside. And if anybody tries to stress me out, what do I do? I just let them go. I don't have time for that. You have to see me driving sometimes. If someone is coming too close to me what do I do? I just move my car to the side. Let them go. After I let two more cars go, I return to the lane. I don't have time for that. I don't want stress.

I was driving one day on the highway and there were cars in front of me. I tell my children also, make sure there is at least one car space between your car and the car ahead of you. That is how I teach them. So I do the same. I don't go too close to the car ahead of me. Maybe the other driver wanted me to go closer. He was so upset, he gave me the finger. I said, "My goodness. What did I do?" Nothing. The guy in front was also slow. He gave the finger again. I told the person in the car with me there would be more than a finger because I know the road. I knew when we got to exit 67, there would be a holdup.

I said, "Let me see how he's going to fly." Just as I thought, there was a holdup. All the fingers stopped. I can just imagine how angry he was. He could not go around the traffic. What if I had lived from the outside? I would have driven close to him and gave him the finger also. Imagine giving fingers back and forth. What sense would it make? Who would benefit?

The well dimension of God's anointing is for you to enjoy your life to the fullest. It's for you.

As you go about your daily life, do not speak your experience. Speak your expectation. If you keep on speaking your experience, you will keep on experiencing your experience. When you start speaking your expectation, your expectation becomes your experience.

If you keep on speaking your experience, you will keep on experiencing your experience, because that is what you've been speaking. What you speak is what you experience. Would you like to experience your expectation? Then speak your expectation. If you want your son to behave well, then speak it. "But I can't say that. I'd be lying." Then keep speaking your experience and see what happens. No progress. Speak what you want to see. Tell your children they are the best children in the world. Call it forth. "You are the most patient son ever." If you keep on saying that, the child will become patient. Don't tell your husband, "You are the worst man ever. Very impatient." Eventually, he may very well become what you profess. You will experience what you speak into existence.

## The River Dimension of the Anointing

Have you ever been to the river? Have you ever jumped into a river?

He that believeth on me, as the scripture hath said, out of his belly shall flow rivers of living water (John 7:38).

The river dimension is a progression from the well to the river. The anointing becomes like a flowing river. Note that the water in a well does not flow. It is stationary. You have to draw from it. However, with the river dimension, there's a flow, no more stagnation.

The purpose of the river anointing is very clear and simple. It is to bring about prosperity and abundance. In case you do not know this, the anointing makes you wealthy. But you can only receive what you believe. Jesus said, "The Spirit of the Lord is upon me for He has anointed me to preach the good news to the poor." What is the best news to the poor? Not to be poor anymore. The anointing of God in the river dimension brings two things:

1. Prosperity/Abundance/Overflow
2. Brings healing

In this dimension of God's anointing, it is not just belief; it is trust and total reliance on God. You need to completely depend on the one who supplies the anointing, the God of heaven who gives power. It requires full trust in this God who gives you everything you need or desire. Trust completely relies and cleaves.

The flow of the river anointing is continuous. Rivers of living water will not stop flowing in a week. The river moves all the time. Perhaps, you are born again, and you are at the well level. Nothing is moving in your life. You are in that state because you are at the well level, nothing flows outward.

You may have started a business at the well level, but it closed down. You may have started something, but it was messed up. Maybe you started to go to school, but you couldn't finish. You started a new job, but you quit in seven weeks. The fact is that you remain stagnant at the well level. However, in the river dimension of God's anointing, whatever you touch prospers. If you start school, you finish. If you start a job or a ministry, you don't quit suddenly because things are getting difficult for you.

It does not matter where you are, once you have the river dimension you will flow in the anointing. Even in the desert, the dark places, and dry seasons of our lives the rivers of water will flow. If you move to Bethlehem, you flow. If you move to Allentown, you still flow because you carry a river dimension. It doesn't matter where you are, it just keeps flowing. It is not about where you are now. It's what you carry. It's about how you are flowing and your ability to release the anointing.

You have to allow the anointing to work for you. But if it's at the well level, you have to constantly draw it out.

Everywhere I go the river flows – river of abundance, healing, and flowing. Everywhere I go, I release the anointing for prosperity and healing. The angels are responsible for bringing prosperity. They are all around me. The angels are responsible for healing. They are all around me because I carry the river dimension of God's anointing!

> And it shall come to pass, that everything that liveth, which moveth, whithersoever the rivers shall come, shall live: and there shall be a very great multitude of fish, because these waters shall come thither: for they shall be healed; and everything shall live whither the river cometh (Ezekiel 47:9).

Do you see that? The Bible says whosoever comes close to the river dimension shall live. And there shall be a great multitude of fish. The fish represents people. Jesus will make us fishers of men and give us life. As we face life's trials and tribulations, God will strengthen and deliver us. If you are sick, you will be healed. If you are depressed, you will be happy.

You may be broke, but God will turn around your financial situation. At a meeting, I felt insulted by the comments of someone who thought he was paying me a compliment. I just shook my head because I knew where I was going. He told somebody, "You know that apostle, his church – the people in his church, they are low-income people; yet, they were able to raise money to build the church. They don't have money. I don't know how they brought the money together." I said, "When you come back here, you will see I'm raising millionaires in this church."

He based his assessment on what he saw back then. When we were a very young church, many of the members of my church did not have cars and jobs. They had very little. However, their lives have changed. Many have their own businesses now. They are prospering because I kept on preaching messages of how the river dimension increases wealth and transforms lives.

Do you want your own house? Do you want a job? Do you want a family? Let this river bring you prosperity. Let there be a supernatural upliftment. Tell everybody you're getting your house next year. Tell your boss. Tell your colleagues. Tell your landlady. Don't worry about the money. That is not an issue. The anointing supplies all your needs.

Everything is dying in your life because there is no river dimension. The river dimension causes everything you touch to live. Wherever the river goes, whoever the river makes contact with, there is always change. The river brings change.

*Declare:*

I will never know lack after today in the name of Jesus.

I will never be broke after today because of the anointing and the river dimension that is about to be released upon my life.

I traveled with one of my children to Nigeria. I preached on, "Having Favor with God and Man." I told my son, "I want to show you what I've been preaching about, how it works." I said, "You're going to experience favor throughout this journey."

We arrived at the airport and the first person he met was one of the pilots. He said, "You are such a handsome young man. What is your name?" My son answered. "What school do you go to?" He told him the school. He said "Listen. This is my card. If you have any 'As,' I'll give you a free trip all around the US." My son was very excited about that.

I told him, "I want you to experience first class, but Daddy will not pay any money for first class. Just watch. I told him, "Say favor." He obeyed.

We went to the airline ticket counter. I said, "Good afternoon, sir. I'm traveling to New York. I told my son that he's going to fly first class today without me paying first class fare."

He looked at me and said, "We don't do that."

I said, "I know, but you will do it this time. There is always a first time."

He said, "But we don't "

I said, "I know that, but I told him you have to. I don't mind if I fly economy, but he has to fly first class. I told him about favor and how favor works. I preached it too, so it must work today."

My son was embarrassed. He said, "Daddy, stop that."

I said, "No this thing works."

The guy kept keying information in the computer. He said,

"The fare to change your flight to first class is over $2,000 for both of you."

I said, "I only want one person."

He said, "Even with one, it's over one thousand dollars."

I said, "Listen. I only have one hundred dollars to spare if at all. Give me what you've got." After searching some more, he brought out two boarding passes for two first class seats. My son and I flew first class for nothing.

> And by the river upon the bank thereof, on this side and on that side, shall grow all trees for meat, whose leaf shall not fade, neither shall the fruit thereof be consumed: it shall bring forth new fruit according to his months, because their waters they issued out of the sanctuary: and the fruit thereof shall be for meat, and the leaf thereof for medicine (Ezekiel 47:12).

See, when you carry this particular anointing, you always have food. If you want chicken, it's there. If you want fish, it's there. If you want rice, it's there. I will never be hungry in my life. The Bible says so (Ezekiel 47:12). I didn't say that, the Bible did, and I believe what it says. It says, "On this side and on that side, shall grow all trees for meat, whose leaf shall not fade, neither shall the fruit thereof be consumed." I mean, you cannot eat so much that there is nothing left because the Bible says, it shall bring forth new fruit every month. Did it say every year? Every month, you have new fruits, why? They are issued out of the sanctuary. Where is the sanctuary? Who is the sanctuary? You are.

Prosperity and healing will come out of you because you carry this river dimension. There is an abundance of resources, and you bring healing to everyone.

The Bible says every month, you are fruitful. So this anointing level brings prosperity and healing. Not just to you, but to others. Those who have contact with you have no choice but to be blessed. If they are depressed, the mere fact that you are issuing rivers will cause depression to get washed off. If they are broke, when they come in contact with you, their lifestyles will get better. If they are sick, when they come into contact with you, they will be healed. Remember, the anointing will produce only when you let it produce.

## Let the anointing produce and flow. Prosperity will come.

Don't stifle it. Healing will flow out of you. Don't keep it to yourself. Step out and release it to somebody. If God tells you pray for that person, go and pray. If God says bless others, go and sow into their lives. The more you release, the more it flows. Are you ready for this dimension? Do you want it?

## The Flood Dimension of the Anointing

This is another dimension of the power of God. Having the flood dimension does not mean you get rid of the river dimension or the well dimension. The well produces the river and the river produces the flood. Without the well, there can be no river. Without the river, there can be no flood.

The Lord spake also unto me again, saying,

> Forasmuch as this people refuseth the waters of Shiloah that go softly, and rejoice in Rezin and Remaliah's son;
>
> Now therefore, behold, the Lord bringeth up upon them the waters of the river, strong and many, even the king of Assyria, and all his glory:

and he shall come up over all his channels, and go over all his banks:

And he shall pass through Judah; he shall over-flow and go over, he shall reach even to the neck; and the stretching out of his wings shall fill the breadth of thy land, O Immanuel (Isaiah 8:5–8).

The Enemy wants us to resist the river level. He knows the benefits to be had. Many times, the Enemy knows you're anointed; you have the river dimension in your life; you bring healing and prosperity. Therefore, he will not let go unless you go to the next stage in your life. In the flood dimension, you will put the Enemy at bay.

The people refused the soft waters of Shiloh. There was a strong overflow. The river dimension was soft, and the Enemy of God resisted it. God decided to bring the next level of the anointing, which is the flood. "The power of God," the Bible says, "will come like a flood over the enemies of God." The flood dimension is for defense protection. It takes you to a place of dominion, where you have divine protection and de-fense over the powers of darkness. Often times, the Enemy will still try to attack you when you are anointed. But when the flood dimension comes upon you, a defense system is installed that works for and in you. Therefore, when the Enemy tries to raise up his ugly head, we should know that he is always defeated. God's divine protection covers you.

David walked in this protection, in this particular anoint-ing. In spite of the Enemy's fierce attacks, David was never defeated. So the flood dimension is very critical. Thus, every child of God must understand how to tap into it. You can walk and do the things God has called you to do.

The flood dimension ensures that nothing stops you from

progressing in every area of your life. It gets to the neck of poverty and anything that tries to come against you. When you walk in this flood dimension, nothing scares you. You do not have to fight. Release the flood anointing and all the Enemy's attacks will return to sender without you saying a word.

> Associate yourselves, O ye people, and ye shall be broken in pieces (Isaiah 8:9).

> Take counsel together, and it shall come to nought; speak the word, and it shall not stand: for God is with you (Isaiah 8:10).

Wherever you are, God is with you. If there is a battle, God is with you. If there are problems around you, God is with you. If people are talking against you, God is with you. Emmanuel means anointing. Again, anointing basically is the overflow of the person of Jesus. When He is with you, no Devil in hell can mess with your territory.

## Declare:

When I go to bed, God is with me.
When I'm driving on the street, God is with me.
When I'm sleeping, God is with me.
When I'm praying, God is with me.
Whatever I am doing, God is with me.
When I'm taking my exams, God is with me.
When I'm at work, God is with me.

## Talk and live boldly!

We are immovable and untouchable. Every Devil is under our feet. Right now, all the demons in this region are subject to me. I can say that because I can say that. I can say that everyone in the Spirit Temple Church will continue to prosper. I can say that because I know it is possible.

> So shall they fear the name of the LORD from the west, and his glory from the rising of the sun. When the enemy shall come in like a flood, the Spirit of the LORD shall lift up a standard against him (Isaiah 59:19).

As I mentioned earlier, commas, periods, and other punctuation marks are not inspired. So if you look at your Bible, it says, "When the Enemy shall come in like a flood, [comma] the Spirit of the Lord ..." Actually that should read: "When the Enemy comes in, like a flood the Spirit of the Lord shall lift up a standard against him." The correct placement of the comma is essential. It changes the entire meaning of this verse.

When the Egyptians pursued the Israelites, God allowed them to be swallowed in the flood. The water just came back together. They were all buried there because they were trying to come against God's people. When you carry this flood dimension, the Enemy will mark you as a dangerous human being. You are a danger to the kingdom of darkness. It doesn't matter if you have five, six, or eight children; don't be afraid. This anointing will cover them also.

> And at midnight Paul and Silas prayed, and sang praises unto God: and the prisoners heard them.

> And suddenly there was a great earthquake, so that the foundations of the prison were shaken: and immediately all the doors were opened, and every one's bands were loosed.

And the keeper of the prison awaking out of his sleep, and seeing the prison doors open, he drew out his sword, and would have killed himself, supposing that the prisoners had been fled.

But Paul cried with a loud voice, saying, Do thyself no harm: for we are all here.

> Then he called for a light, and sprang in, and
> came trembling, and fell down before Paul and
> Silas (Acts 16:25–29).

Two men who were operating in the flood anointing dimension were praying and when the earthquake hit, everybody was free. That is what a flood dimension can do. As Christians, we carry this mandate. The flood dimension of God's power will work for you. The earthquake is about to take place now. Things are about to break loose. The chains of poverty are about to be broken. The chains of sickness are about to be broken. The chains of depression are about to be broken. The chains of family and generational curses are about to be broken. That disease that killed your grandma is about to be broken. You will not die another man's death. You will not die the death of your father. You will not die the death of your grandpa.

The flood anointing is available to every believer who desires more. God will fill your life to the overflowing. Are you longing for the fullness? Then bring your vessel, your life and claim the unfailing promises of God.

# Chapter 13

## The Secrets of the Anointing

We understand that the anointing of God is the power of the Holy Spirit working in our lives to do great exploits. His anointing is upon our lives for ministry and service. God wants every one of us to carry His power.

> But ye shall receive power, after that the Holy Ghost is come upon you: and ye shall be witnesses unto me both in Jerusalem, and in all Judaea, and in Samaria, and unto the uttermost part of the earth (Acts 1:8).

God wants all believers to have the dunamis working in their lives. The anointing God puts upon your life does wonderful things for you. Equally so, God uses you to do great things in the lives of others.

A secret is something you don't yet know. You don't understand how to appropriate it in your life. I will share the secrets of tapping into or receiving God's anointing upon our lives. God's anointing upon your life is like pregnancy. It cannot be hidden. You may try to hide it for a little bit but eventually, it shows. Everyone knows you are carrying a new life.

Right now, you carry something. It's like a jacket. When

135

you put it on or when God puts it on you, there is a radical change. In fact, when God puts it on you, you cease to be you.

When I am ministering, I'm in the service of God. I cease to be Ese Duke. It is better for you to know me in the spirit because trying to know me in the flesh, as good as that is, shouldn't be too much of your interest. You want to know me in the spirit because the spirit is what works wonders in our lives. You cannot receive a lot from me if you want to be buddy, buddy with me. You've got to begin to see the spirit of God working in the life of the man of God.

Just in case you don't know it, you are a minister of God. God said, I have given you the ministry of reconciliation – reconciling other people to God. The Bible says you shall receive power after the Holy Ghost has come upon you so you can do your ministry of witnessing (Acts 1:8). You shall receive power after the Holy Ghost has come upon you so that you can be witnesses. Witnessing is a ministry. God wants you to be a witness. He wants you to talk about Him, to demonstrate His power, and once you are anointed by the Holy Ghost, once that anointing upon your life begins to manifest, you become a real witness.

You don't even have to talk too much. You just tell people, "Jesus loves you." You say, "Come, I'm going to pray for you right now. And you're going to see the power of God move in your life because Jesus loves you. And if you believe in Jesus, He will do this and this for you." Whatever you speak from your mouth is fulfilled because you have the anointing on your life. If you think it's only for the pastors, you got it wrong. You can carry God's anointing on your life.

The secret is very simple. It's a desire and hunger in your heart to be anointed. How hungry are you for the anointing? How much do you really want to be anointed? What are you willing to let go to be anointed? God wants to anoint you, God wants to put His power in your life, but do you desire it? Do you really want it? How much do you desire God's anointing on your life? How much of God's power do you want in your life?

Some of you say, "Oh, God, I thank you. The man of God is anointed, that's all I need. I just need the man of God's anointing on my life." As much as that is good, you need more than that. God wants to anoint you. Are you following me? He wants you to carry His power also even if it's just a little bit of it. A little is better than nothing.

*Having a little of God's power is better than having none.*

> As the hart panteth after the water brooks, so panteth my soul after thee, O God (Psalm 42:1).

Your hunger makes a big difference. It will determine if God will anoint you. It will tell if God will put His mantle on you. The level of anointing upon your life is not God's prerogative. It is yours. It is your desire. God cannot give you what you don't want. He cannot put His anointing upon you if it doesn't even cross your mind. No, it is what you desire that He will put on your life.

> Ho, every one that thirsteth, come ye to the waters, and he that hath no money; come ye, buy, and eat; yea, come, buy wine and milk without money and without price (Isaiah 55:1).

Eternal life has no price to it. You just come and receive. However, thirst comes with the anointing. God's anointing upon your life has a price but your desire of that anointing can release the hand of God to put His power upon you.

> For I will pour water upon him that is thirsty, and floods upon the dry ground: I will pour my spirit upon thy seed, and my blessing upon thine offspring (Isaiah 44:3).

Elisha deeply desired a double portion of the anointing from his master. This is what he was living for. That's what he wanted more than anything in his life.

> And it came to pass, when they were gone over, that Elijah said unto Elisha, Ask what I shall do for thee, before I be taken away from thee. And Elisha said, I pray thee, let a double portion of thy spirit be upon me (2 Kings 2:9).

Elisha said, "Let a double portion of thy spirit be upon me." Let that sink in. He wanted a double portion of Elijah's spirit to rest upon him because the Holy Spirit can only anoint you to the extent of the capacity of your spirit.

> And he said, Thou hast asked a hard thing: nevertheless, if thou see me when I am taken from thee, it shall be so unto thee; but if not, it shall not be so (2 Kings 2:10).

How do you deal with the anointing that you are exposed to? Do you respect the anointing you are exposed to? Do you honor the anointing that God has put in your life? Do you respect the anointing and the anointed of God that He has positioned in your midst? Elisha said, "I want a double portion of what you've got, of what is in you." The same thing happened to Moses. God took some of Moses' anointing and gave it to the 70 elders. God will put somebody in your life to impart His anointing on you. However, you must have a desire for what is on that person's life to rest upon your life.

Have you seen God with your natural eyes? You have not, but you have seen a man of God who carries the anointing with your natural eyes. It is what you see that can manifest in your life. If you can see it, you can have it. If you cannot see it, you cannot have it. It all stems from a desire in your spirit.

I remember as a young man, I desired so much to be anointed like my pastor. I wanted to be like him. I tried to talk like him. I tried to walk like him. I tried to dress like him. I just wanted what he had. Anywhere he was speaking, I was right there sitting down. And I began to pray: I began to desire this thing. I said "God, if you can just give me a little bit. If you can just anoint me with something that you put on this man. If you can just anoint me." I prayed and I prayed until God put a very strong desire in my heart. I said, "God. I need more." And I began to pray and fast. And I said, "God. I will not break this fast until I see your tangible touch on my life." I was hungry.

Paul was blinded by the glory of God, Jesus was right there. Jesus could not open the eyes of Paul. Jesus said, "Paul. I'm sending you to another man to open your eyes for you." And Paul went to a man by the name of Ananias. Ananias said, "Paul receive the Holy Ghost" and immediately, the scales on his eyes fell off. Jesus never said, "Give him the Holy Ghost." Rather, Jesus told Ananias, "Open his eyes." Ananias said, "Receive ye, the Holy Ghost. Your eyes are open."

A young man came for prayer because he had foot drop. Being filled with the anointing, I told him to take his shoes off and lay down. Then I told him to get up and walk. He got up and walked perfectly fine. The foot drop completely stopped. His hip was okay. He walked and he ran. He walked home without his cane and brace. Now that is the power of God in action and every believer can do that with God's power on his/her life.

With the anointing, you can also cast out demons. I did that one Friday with a fourteen year old girl who was demon possessed. All I had to do was go close to her and that was it. The Devil was afflicting her with stomach issues and He could not stand me getting close to her. That day she was healed from the chronic stomachache caused by the Devil. I knew it was spiritual but her parents stopped coming to church regularly. After seven months of being free from the problem, the stomachache started. I told the parents, "If your child is to remain healthy, you must be in the house of God. You cannot stay home because this issue is spiritual. Get her in the environment of the Holy Spirit and the Devil will not stand it." I walked close to her and I could tell something was happening. I put my hands on her and the Devil got scared. I commanded that Devil of stomach pain to leave that girl alone. We knew that right there and then, something miraculous took place. The anointing.

# Chapter 14

## Functions of the Anointing

Once you understand the anointing and function in it, your life can never be the same again. Never! Many people walk around proclaiming to be Christians for many years. However, when you look at their lives, you can tell for a fact that they are not operating in the anointing God has put in them. By their speech and actions, you can tell they are not walking in power. They just say it. "Talk is cheap." You can sing, "Walking in power, walking in miracle. I live a life of favor. I know who I am." It's a lovely song, but if you don't walk in it, it's just talk.

The anointing upon you empowers you to speak specifically to situations. For example, one young girl came to our church and I said, "By June twelfth, this will happen. By August sixteenth, this will happen." Did it happen? Yes. I spoke it into existence. She had not spoken to her father for years. They had a bad relationship. The Lord said, "Speak into her life" and I said, "By June twelfth, your life will start turning around." I said, "By August sixteenth, you're going to get a job in a warehouse." And she got a job. Where? In a warehouse. On what day? August sixteenth. The point I am establishing is that when the man of God releases a prophetic word, everything must work together to make sure that word does not fall to the ground. Otherwise, it looks like God is not doing what He is supposed to do.

If you really have the hunger for the anointing that's effective, you will pray and follow the steps in the Bible that will take you to the place where God can trust you. It's about trust. Can God trust you? Can He trust you with your time? Can He trust you with your money? If He cannot trust you with the 10 percent of your income, how can He trust you with power? Do you know you can do evil with it?

> Whereunto I am ordained a preacher, and an apostle, (I speak the truth in Christ, and lie not ;) a teacher of the Gentiles in faith and verity (1 Timothy 2:7).

> Whereunto I am appointed a preacher, and an apostle, and a teacher of the Gentiles (2 Timothy 1:11).

> But unto every one of us is given grace according to the measure of the gift of Christ (Ephesians 4:7).

> And he gave some, apostles; and some, prophets; and some, evangelists; and some, pastors and teachers;

For the perfecting of the saints, for the work of the ministry, for the edifying of the body of Christ (Ephesians 4:11, 12).

In the above verses, the ministry gifts are listed. Everyone is not a pastor, apostle, prophet, teacher or evangelist. We are not all called to the fivefold ministry. However, we have all been called into some sort of ministry or the other. To function in that ministry effectively, you need the anointing upon your life. Some of you may have the ministry of giving, which is the grace to give.

In the ministry of giving, God gives you the grace and the anointing to make more wealth so you can give because that is your ministry of giving. You need the grace because sometimes, the Enemy will tell you, "Well, don't give anymore. There is enough giving." But God gives the grace and places an anointing upon your life so you can generate wealth and give continuously. You cannot give what you don't have. No matter how much you want to. You can say I wish I could give you a car. If you don't have a car, you can't give a car. Therefore, you need the grace of God upon your life. In fact, the Bible says it is God who gives you the power to make wealth. The "power" in that scripture refers to the anointing.

There is also an anointing to prosper, one for healing, service, to open businesses, to have companies everywhere. With God's anointing upon your life, you can put your hands upon what God has anointed you to do and each time, you prosper without stress.

God has not called you to be a benchwarmer. God has called you to do His work. And to do the work of the ministry, you need the anointing upon your life. The anointing that is in you helps you. It's for you. The one inside is yours. The one upon you is for others to do the ministry work, to serve others. But while you are serving others, you know what? You benefit because you cannot give to others if you don't have it first. So you're still blessed. You cannot be praying for others to get healed if you are sick. It stands to reason, therefore, that if you have the anointing for healing, you have to stay healthy. How can you pray that God will give someone brand new knees when you can hardly lift your knees. Your knees are worn out but you are praying, "God, heal their knees, in the name of Jesus." How about your knees?

God is not going to give you an anointing upon your life if you're going to use that anointing to just sit at home and watch TV. Give up some friends, your leisure, some of the things you like to do, places you like to go, getting angry at the little things and even give up your rights. Once you have the anointing upon you, you have no more rights; it affects your everyday life. Therefore, even when you are driving, you have no rights either because you are operating under a different law. You cannot afford to be upset. You cannot afford to be bitter. You cannot afford to say bad words. You cannot afford to do anything bad anymore. You can't afford to lie and cheat. Why? The Holy Spirit can read your mind. So if you want to think of something bad, He says, "I'm here." Are you ready for that change?

> And the men of Judah came, and there they anointed David king over the house of Judah. And they told David, saying, That the men of Jabeshgilead were they that buried Saul (2 Samuel 2:4).

David had the anointing upon him.

> So all the elders of Israel came to the king to Hebron; and king David made a league with them in Hebron before the Lord: and they anointed David king over Israel (2 Samuel 5:3).

The anointing upon your life is not just a one-time event; it can happen over and over again. God keeps on adding different levels of anointing upon your life. The anointing upon my life is at a different level from when I started. It has increased.

There are different types of the anointing of grace. There is grace for salvation, grace for ministry, and grace for operation.

Every child of God has the grace for salvation. This is the anointing to save you. Once you are saved, you have that anointing on you, so you have the grace for salvation. Every minister does not operate in the same grace.

Do you know what grace is? Favor. Grace brings ease. I love it. I say it all the time because I'm living in the grace of God. If you are a student, your school life is easy. If you are married, your marriage is easy. "Oh, but pastor, Jesus Christ said I must suffer so I am for suffering." Do you want to suffer? Haven't you suffered enough? I've suffered enough. Let me enjoy ease now. There was a time I suffered. I can't suffer forever. No way! Let me enjoy this life. I have tasted both lives; this one is better. I'm not going back to the other one. No, the life of ease is much sweeter.

> The enemy shall not exact upon him; nor the
> son of wickedness afflict him (Psalm 89:22).

Wickedness can no longer afflict you. The Enemy cannot oppress you because you are hidden in the rock. The son of wickedness cannot afflict you because you are anointed.

There should be a difference between you and the person on the street because you carry the mantle of God. You have God's anointing, not only in you but upon your life. You may not be at the top level, but, at least, you've got something. Something is better than nothing. And you can learn how to increase what you have. The more faithful and dependent you are on the Holy Ghost, and the more you follow these steps that I am sharing with you, the more that anointing of God upon your life will increase. You will reach a place without measure.

As Christians, we need to experience the anointing of the Holy Ghost, not only read about it in a book. Our lives must demonstrate the anointing on a daily basis. When you begin to tap into grace, you begin to flow in the level of anointing upon your life that you would never have imagined. You might have seen people flowing in that same anointing and wondered, "My God, how come I cannot operate like that?" Now, you have a little piece of it in and upon your life. You can walk towards the Devil and he will run away from you. You don't have to say a word because you have put on the jacket, the mantle.

The anointing takes you to a place that is very different. It makes you a different person. When that mantle is heavy on me, I am not the same. My eyes change. One day, I watched a video and the person didn't look like me at all. Usually, I love to smile and laugh but when that anointing is upon me, it seems like I can break a wall and go through it. I have so much power. It is very strong. I cannot even describe what I am feeling or what is happening. God wants all His children to have that experience – including you.

# Chapter 15

## Growing in the Anointing

It is very important to know that we can grow in the anointing.

> And these signs shall follow them that believe; In my name shall they cast out devils; they shall speak with new tongues;
>
> They shall take up serpents; and if they drink any deadly thing, it shall not hurt them; they shall lay hands on the sick, and they shall recover (Mark 16:17–18).

Don't accept the lie that the abilities outlined in the above scripture refer only to the disciples two thousand years ago. Today, many propagate that everything has changed and with technology, Christianity is different. That's not true. It's just an excuse. They say these things because they don't see signs and wonders in their lives. However, rather than making frivolous excuses, you should learn how to change your life to manifest the power of God.

As a Christian, you have to ask yourself these pertinent questions, "What am I doing or what am I not doing to stop the revelation of God's power in me? The Bible says, 'The Lord is my shepherd. I shall not want,' so why am I always in need?" Clearly, a problem exists. God is not a man that He should lie. He is not the Son of man that He should change His mind. Has He said it and will He not do it? God backs up everything He says.

"You shall lay your hands on the sick and they will recover." How come many Christians lay their hands on the sick and the sick get sicker? Or lay hands on themselves and never recover. Some people are scared of letting certain believers pray for them because they think they will get even worse. That means there is something wrong with what some of us are doing. On the other hand some Christians lay their hands on the sick and the sick recover. Some Christians cast out devils.

Have you ever cast out a devil? Do they have two heads or one head? Do they have four hands or two hands? Do they have more than twenty four hours in a day? Do they have anything different from anybody else? I asked those questions to point out that those who cast out devils and pray for the sick to recover are human beings just like you. They are believers just like you. So how come they cast out devils but you run when the Devil appears? Something has happened in their lives that has not occurred in yours. But I pray that as you understand the anointing in you can grow, you will be able to cast out devils confidently.

Some people come to me and say, "Pastor, I tried to cast out a devil, but he did not leave. Jesus Christ said this type doesn't go out except by prayer and fasting. So I'm going to pray and fast first for a week before I come back to cast out the Devil." That is still wrong. You must always read the Bible in the light of Jesus. Was it said before the cross or after the cross? Before the cross, the Devil still had some powers.

But Jesus Christ went to the grave and "disarmed" Him. He took away Satan's power. He stripped him and made him a public disgrace.

Where I grew up, if you were caught stealing, they would put a sign around your neck. The entire town would play a drum, and they would parade you through the street shouting, "He is a criminal." They would sing a song and parade you in the streets. In other words, they made you a public disgrace. The entire town would know you were caught stealing.

Jesus Christ paraded the Devil and showed the entire world, the underworld, and the spirit realm, that he has been defeated and disgraced. So the Devil has no power except the power you give to him by what you say.

The Devil is not after your money. He is not after your cars. He is not even after your husband or your wife. He's not. He's after your words. If he can get your words, he has got you. That's why you must not give him your word. Don't say the things he wants you to say because once you do, you give him authority to do the things you never wanted to happen in your life.

The Devil does not have a legal right on this planet earth. This is a planet for human beings who have spirits and bodies. Not just a spirit. The Holy Spirit is not floating around. He lives in a person. That is the only way He can be here. This world, this earth was given to man. Jesus Christ took it back from the Devil and returned it to the hands of man. That's you. So the Devil has no right on this planet, except you invite him to your house. Unless you say, "Oh, the Devil is always after me; he's after me." You just said it. Now, you've given him the authority to come after you. You say, "Oh, my God, he's messing with my family?" You just told him to do that. Or you say, "Oh, my goodness, I don't understand it. The Devil is constantly messing with me." You just said it.

Now you have allowed him to do the things he could not do. Since you released it, you've given him the authority to do it.

Watch everything you say because the power is in your mouth. It is the same thing with the Holy Spirit. As powerful as God is, He cannot force His will on you. God cannot make you do what you don't want to do. That's why He said in His Word, "I present before you life and death." He said, "But please choose life so you can live" (Deuteronomy 30:19). If you don't yield to the Holy Spirit, He cannot reside in you. You have to invite Him into your heart. So before the cross, Jesus Christ said, "This kind of devil does not go out unless by prayer and fasting." But right now, after the cross, you can tell any devil to leave and he will.

You don't need to fast for the Devil. Eat your food and cast out the Devil. Command Satan to leave. He will leave. The power is in your mouth.

"All power has been given to Jesus." He said, "Behold, I give you power over all of the authority of the devil and nothing shall by any means hurt you." Many Christians quote that scripture and all they see is, "I give you power over all the powers of the Enemy." But that was before the cross. After the cross, the Enemy has no more power. He said, the weapons of our warfare are not carnal. But they are mighty through God to the pulling down of strongholds. He also said, "Casting down all imaginations." The battlefield is in your mind. If you think the Devil has you, he does.

Many Christians are unable to do what they are supposed to because the anointing in them needs to grow. The anointing in this sense is defined as the power of God working in your life. I am not saying that the Spirit of God needs to grow. The Spirit of God is the same Spirit. The Spirit of God in you is not in quantity. You do not have a big Holy Spirit and small Holy Spirit. It's the same Holy Ghost. The important factor is how much of its power can be released in you. That's why it is critical that you let the anointing of God in you grow.

You must stand on your exousia/ authority and command the Devil to leave. If he doesn't, repeat it again because some devils want to test your authority. Like some of you have children who test your authority. They want to see if Mommy and Daddy will really stand by what they say. Don't back down. Once he knows you are serious, he will leave.

> In the last day, that great day of the feast, Jesus stood and cried, saying, If any man thirst, let him come unto me, and drink.
>
> He that believeth on me, as the scripture hath said, out of his belly shall flow rivers of living water.
>
> But this spake he of the Spirit, which they that believe on him should receive: for the Holy Ghost was not yet given; because that Jesus was not yet glorified (John 7:37–39).

The Holy Spirit lives in you as a child of God. But the flow of the river in you is dependent on some factors. The river is in you, but whether it's flowing or not depends on you. The flow can be clogged up based on some things in your life. The Devil challenges your authority because the flow is blocked.

> Having then gifts differing according to the grace that is given to us, whether prophecy, let us prophesy according to the proportion of faith (Romans 12:6).

Here we see that we have different gifts according to the

grace given to each of us. If your gift is prophesying then prophesy in accordance with your faith; if it is serving, then serve. If it is teaching, then teach. If it is to encourage, then give encouragement. If it is giving, then give generously. If it is to lead, do it diligently. If it is to show mercy, do it cheerfully. The previous scripture shows that the anointing within us can grow, unlike what many are falsely teaching.

As believers, we can grow in faith. So if you can grow in the faith, the power of God in you can grow also. Remember, releasing the anointment of God within you depends on two factors: the spoken word and faith. So the anointing within can grow if you grow in faith.

> We are bound to thank God always for you, brethren, as it is meet, because that your faith groweth exceedingly, and the charity of every one of you all toward each other aboundeth (2 Thessalonians 1:3).

Paul writes to the Thessalonica Christians saying he's thankful to God because they are growing in faith, "And your love for each other is increasing." The growth of your faith is directly proportionate to the growth of God's anointing within you. I reiterate, the anointing within you can grow. It should not be stagnant, but if you don't know it can grow, you will settle for mediocrity. Also, you don't have to wait for the anointing upon you if you can learn how to grow the anointing within.

> But grow in grace, and in the knowledge of our Lord and Saviour Jesus Christ. To him be glory both now and forever. Amen (2 Peter 3:18).

We can grow in grace. You cannot operate in the gift of

God or in God's anointing any higher than your level of faith or grace. The more faith you have, the more intensity the anointing within you and the more you will realize God's grace in your life.

> Grace and peace be multiplied unto you through the knowledge of God, and of Jesus our Lord (2 Peter 1:2).

> And we all, who with unveiled faces contemplate the Lord's glory, are being transformed into his image with ever-increasing glory, which comes from the Lord, who is the Spirit (2 Corinthians 3:18, NIV).

There is an increase in the glorification of God's people. The more God's glory is manifest in your life, the more of the anointing within you will reveal in your life.

So the growth in glory produces growth in the believers anointing. Allow the glory and presence of God to grow more in you. In other words, be conscious of God's presence in your life. The more you are conscious of God's presence and glory, the more the anointing is released in you. So if you can grow in glory, grace, and faith, you can grow in the anointing. When you increase in glory, when you're conscious of the presence of God all the time, the anointing within you is much more powerful.

What is grace? Favor of God. How do you grow? Where is God's favor? God's favor is found in God's presence. If you want His favor, get in His presence. Without His presence, there is no favor. God's power is also found in God's presence. If you want His power, get in His presence. Without His presence, there is no power. So ultimately, if you want to have an increase in the anointing within you, get in the presence of God found in the Holy of Holies. Not in the outer court. Not in the inner court but in the Holy of Holies.

Do you believe you can grow in the anointing? Are you ready to grow in the anointing so that can cast out devils? So that when the Devil tries to attack your children, you can command him to leave in the name of Jesus. Some time ago, my daughter was having issue with her face that was distressing her. I laid my hands on her and commanded the Devil to go. Soon after, her skin was clear. As she saw the power of God revealed in her life practically, she started to desire coming to church. The child who would make excuses about having homework and having to drive a long distance to get to church, now comes more regularly. You see, we need the power of God to ward off the attacks of the Devil on our children. When the power of God is in you, you don't have to wait to call the apostle in the early hours of the morning or the late hours of the night for prayers.

As Christian, we need to fast. I believe in fasting. But don't waste your time fasting because of the Devil. You fast because you want to get something from God. Don't put the Devil in that place. Put him down. You are not fighting a war. The Devil has been defeated. You are only establishing your authority over him. You're not fighting. People tell you about warfare fighting. When will you stop fighting? If you keep fighting for your life when will you enjoy living? You've been fighting ever since you've been born again. When will you enjoy your Christian life? Believe me; I've done the same thing, too. So I'm not just telling you. I've done it. I have waged war on the Devil. I have prepared for Devil. But I have come to realize that the Devil has been defeated. Why should I spend a whole month fighting the Devil who has been defeated already. It's ignorance. It is a disease. My people perish for lack of knowledge.

If you need to fast, do so because God asks you to fast and because you want to have a very high sensitivity of your spirit man to what God is telling you, not what the Devil is talking. Your heightened hearing is not to hear the Devil's voice. If you hear a devil's voice all day, something is wrong. Tune your ears to the Spirit of God. That's how you will grow. Many times, when you fast because God asks you to fast, you can hear Him speak very clearly.

At one point in my ministry, before I preached on Sundays, I would not eat. Before healing services, I used to go three days straight fasting. Wednesday, Thursday, Friday, I would eat no food. My eyes looked different. I could not wait to say, "Amen." But that was for God, not because of the Devil. I can cast out devils anytime. I realized I was more spiritually sensitive when I fasted. I was more accurate when I fasted. But the time came when I had to stop depending on that so it didn't seem as if it was only because I was fasting that God was moving. So one time, I said, "God, I'm not going to fast. I was going to do as led. And that time, God moved so much, I realized He was not moving because I fasted but because He wanted to.

# Chapter 16

## How to Put a Demand on the Anointing

W here there is a demand, there is a supply. The anointing breaks the yoke of bondage, disease, poverty, demonic oppression, and calamities.

The anointing brings healing, deliverance, prosperity, and all the things you desire in your life. You must put a demand on the anointing to receive supply in your life.

> And it shall come to pass in that day, that his burden shall be taken away from off thy shoulder, and his yoke from off thy neck, and the yoke shall be destroyed because of the anointing (Isaiah 10:27).

If you don't put a demand on the anointing, there will be no release of that particular anointing in your life. You can be in a room with God's power moving mightily but until you put a demand on the anointing, you won't receive what belongs to you. How do you put a demand on this anointing? How do I put a demand on the anointing of God that is upon the life of the man of God?

## Faith

Without faith, it is impossible to please God. Faith is the channel through which the anointing flows. Faith is like a light switch that turns on the anointing to flow into your life. If you don't believe, you have no faith. The anointing can be very strong in your church, but you would just be a spectator, not a participator. I pray that you will not only look at those who are receiving miracles, but you will be one of those who receive miracles.

Turn on that switch, and let the power of God flow into your life. A woman visited our church with her son who had a problem with his liver. He had a distended abdomen and struggled with that for some time. But I knew that his mother had faith. I put that child against my abdomen and released the power of God to that child. Not long after, the mother and the father sent me more than a five page letter with pictures of their son after prayer. The child was healed. God is great!

God is so powerful. You have to believe and have faith in God and in the man of God as he declares healing and deliverance by faith. Why does God have to use man? God believes in man. God could have saved the world with the snap of the finger, but He sent Jesus in the form of a man. Saul had an encounter with Jesus and Saul became blind. In spite of Jesus' power, He did not remove the scales from the eyes of Saul. He told Saul to go and meet a man who would take the scales from his eyes. In our culture, sometimes, we don't understand why God would use a man. We think the man is a mere mortal. We fail to understand, he is not just a man but a man of God.

Saul went over to Ananias who prayed and the scales fell from the eyes of Saul. Ananias, being a very nice, kind man said, "Receive the Holy Ghost." And Saul received the Holy Ghost. A man spoke into the life of another man. So don't underestimate the power that is in the man of God; he speaks life into your spirit, circumstances, and situations.

> And it came to pass on a certain day, as he was teaching, that there were Pharisees and doctors of the law sitting by, which were come out of every town of Galilee, and Judaea, and Jerusalem: and the power of the Lord was present to heal them.

> And, behold, men brought in a bed a man which was taken with a palsy: and they sought means to bring him in, and to lay him before him.

> And when they could not find by what way they might bring him in because of the multitude, they went upon the housetop, and let him down through the tiling with his couch into the midst before Jesus.

> And when he saw their faith, he said unto him, Man, thy sins are forgiven thee.

> And the scribes and the Pharisees began to reason, saying, Who is this which speaketh blasphemies? Who can forgive sins, but God alone?

> But when Jesus perceived their thoughts, he answering said unto them, What reason ye in your hearts?

> Whether is easier, to say, Thy sins be forgiven thee; or to say, Rise up and walk?

But that ye may know that the Son of man hath power upon earth to forgive sins, (he said unto the sick of the palsy,) I say unto thee, Arise, and take up thy couch, and go into thine house (Luke 5:17–24).

Jesus was teaching in the midst of Pharisees and doctors of the law who came out of every town of Galilee, Judea, and Jerusalem. The power of God was present to heal. In spite of their knowledge, they were not healed. Some men brought a man who had palsy, and they tried to lay him before Jesus. But they could not find a way through the crowd. So these men opened up the roof and lowered their friend who was paralyzed, in the presence of Jesus.

When Jesus saw their faith, He said, "Man, thy sins be forgiven thee." Back then, as people do now, they equated sickness to sin. Jesus told this man to arise and immediately, he got up, took up his bed, and glorified God. The people around were all amazed and glorified God as well. They were filled with fear saying, "We have not seen this kind of thing before." Strange things happen when God's anointing is demanded.

*Believe all things are possible and receive your miracle.*

And a certain woman, which had an issue of blood twelve years,

And had suffered many things of many physicians, and had spent all that she had, and was nothing bettered, but rather grew worse,

When she had heard of Jesus, came in the press behind, and touched his garment.

For she said, If I may touch but his clothes, I shall be whole.

And straightway the fountain of her blood was dried up; and she felt in her body that she was healed of that plague.

And Jesus, immediately knowing in himself that virtue had gone out of him, turned him about in the press, and said, Who touched my clothes?

And his disciples said unto him, Thou seest the multitude thronging thee, and sayest thou, Who touched me?

And he looked round about to see her that had done this thing.

But the woman fearing and trembling, knowing what was done in her, came and fell down before him, and told him all the truth.

And he said unto her, Daughter, thy faith hath made thee whole; go in peace, and be whole of thy plague (Mark 5:25–34).

A certain woman had a blood disease for twelve years. She suffered many things at the hands of doctors and spent all of her life savings. 401K and all the retirement money were spent but nothing improved. Rather, she grew worse. It reminds me of a young man who came to church. He was experiencing immigration problems and was waiting to be deported. He had already spent thousands of dollars on lawyers. One lawyer told him, "I cannot help you. Nobody in this world can help you because your case cannot be changed."

This man attended my church and brought the letter from immigration to me. He believed in the anointing. He came with his mother and his two children. I said, "You know what? I'm not a lawyer, but I'm going to respond to the immigration officers as your lawyer. I will write three sentences and God's anointing on that paper. They will change their minds." This young man believed. I wrote the three sentences and told the young man not to open the envelope. He sealed it and put it in the mail. To cut a long story short, the immigration responded with an over twenty page letter saying why they must give him his green card.

The woman with the issue of blood said, "If I may touch but his garment, I shall be whole." She touched the hem of Jesus' garment and straight away, the fountain of her blood dried up, and she felt in her body that she was healed of that plague. Immediately, Jesus said, "Somebody touched me because I sensed the power had just left my body." This woman had an agenda. Healing was in demand. She wanted to be made whole.

One day, I was preaching, and unexpectedly, Pastor Gladys took my handkerchief from my hand like it was hers. I was surprised because she is not one to grab my handkerchief. I did not know she had a plan. She was told she had a lump in her breast. I found out she would use the handkerchief every day; she would put it under her breast believing that the anointing from the man of God would melt that lump. She went for a checkup and the doctors told her the lump disappeared. She put a demand on the anointing.

- The woman with the issue of blood was healed against the odds.
- She had many obstacles in her way and several things going against her.
- She was bleeding. The blood must have been smelling.
- She was a woman; thus, she was not allowed to be among men. With the problem she had, she was not allowed to be in the public.
- She was considered unclean, and she could have been put to death if she was caught.

In spite of all that was going against her, the woman said to herself, you know what, I don't care. I'm getting my miracle. And she went against all odds. She went right into the midst of the people. She could barely stand. She must have crawled on her knees just to get to Jesus. She must have faced the ridicule of people just to accomplish her feat. She was willing to take chances; she was willing to dive in because she knew exactly what she wanted.

Her story is one of great expectations against the odds. You too can expect God to heal and deliver you. Expectation is the breeding ground for miracles. Put the demand on the anointing. Behold and declare your healing, deliverance, and change:

- I will get my healing
- I will get my miracle
- I will get my signs and wonders
- I will get my deliverance
- Prosperity will manifest in my life

# Chapter 17

## How to Keep the Anointing Flowing

*I*n the previous chapters, we established the significance of the anointing on and in our lives. We also determined that if our work for God is to be effective, the anointing has to be present. The Holy Spirit's power must be present to bring healing and change. Therefore, every believer who seriously wants to produce in the kingdom has to maintain the flow of the anointing. But how is that done?

### Examine Your Heart: Fear Not

The first order Elijah gave to the widow woman was related to maintaining the correct attitude.

> And Elijah said unto her, Fear not; go and do as thou hast said: but make me thereof a little cake first, and bring it unto me, and after make for thee and for thy son (1 Kings 17:13).

First, you must not be afraid of losing your anointing. You must not be scared of losing the fire. Fear causes you to lose the fire of God in your life. It is a paralyzing spirit.

For God hath not given us the spirit of fear; but
of power, and of love, and of a sound mind (2
Timothy 1:7).

Fear must not be a part of your life. Don't be afraid and
doubt. Instead, be bold and courageous. Believe with all of
your heart that God's power in your life will stay there forever.

On this life's journey, many Christians have doubts: "How
long will this last? How long can this power stay in me?" When
you are prayed for and the power of God comes on you, it is
supposed to stay on you. It's not just for that moment.

As I explained earlier, many years ago when God visited
me and anointed me powerfully, the first thing I did was to
go home and try it out. Likewise, you should try out your
anointing. Go to your neighbors. Try it in Walmart, Kmart,
Giant and other stores. If you really believe you've got the
fire, lay hands on somebody on the streets. It does not have
to be in the church. Go out there. Call your roommate. Call
your colleagues at work. Tell somebody who is sick, "Let me
lay hands on you. I've got the power of God in me." If nothing happens, keep praying. It shows you've got some faith
in you. It means you are not afraid. Expect miracles to take
place because God's power is already in your life and you
must put it to work.

You must eliminate any fear of losing what God has given
to you. You don't have to wait until you go to church to tell
somebody, "The Lord said." Tell the people on the streets,
"The Lord said."

If you are in your church and you believe that God has
given you a prophetic gift, if you believe the Lord showed
you something, tell your pastor. He will let you know if you
should say it or not because it may not be the right time to
do so. Don't go and tell the sister, "The Lord said you should
buy a red shoe." And then, "The Lord said you should buy a

pinkish, red shoe." Then further complicate the situation by saying, "The Lord said you should buy pinkish, reddish, bluish shoes." She will be confused because of too many voices. If you believe you have the gift of God in your life, go out on the street and meet someone on the street and tell them whatever the Lord tells you. If you do not know the person and what you say to them is true, his faith will grow, and he will want to know who you are and how you got it done. That gives you the perfect opportunity to introduce him to Jesus. That is the way it works. That is how you release God's power in your life on others.

Don't be afraid to use your gift, but at the same time, use it appropriately. Practice what God has put in you. Go out of your comfort zone.

## Establish Your Life Priority: Put God First.

The second recommendation Elijah made to this woman addresses priority. The woman told Elijah her problem and Elijah had an interesting response.

> Elijah said to her, "Don't be afraid. Go home and do as you have said. But first make a small loaf of bread for me from what you have and bring it to me, and then make something for yourself and your son (1 King 17:13, NIV).

The word "first" is significant in this passage. If you want God's power to keep flowing in your life, you must put Him first. He must be your priority. He must be number one in your decision making. He should not come after your children's education, your wife's birthday or your best friend's graduation party.

Making God your first priority applies to every area of your life besides just the anointing of God. If you put God first in your finances, you'll be blessed financially. If you put Him first in your marriage, you'll be blessed in your marriage. If you put God first in your health, you'll be blessed in your health. If you put God first in everything that you do, you will be blessed abundantly.

> But seek ye first the kingdom of God, and his righteousness; and all these things shall be added unto you (Matthew 6:33).

Elijah may appear to have been very insensitive because he wanted the widow to give him all she had. Let's say you only had enough money to buy medication for your dying child and the prophet said, "Give that money to God." Would you? Wouldn't you think the prophet is very insensitive? However, from this story, we can see that when you put God first, when you make Him your priority, great things begin to happen in your life.

As insensitive and selfish Elijah's request sounded the old woman obeyed and reaped the rewards. After giving all that she had, she received more than she could ever have imagined. As a matter of fact, she had a constant supply. There was no lack. She had enough food to feed the prophet, her son and herself as long as it was needed.

If you want God's power in your life and the fire of God to keep on burning in you, make God your priority.

When Elisha was called by his master Elijah. He said, "Let me go first and take care of some home business." Elijah said, "No! Follow me."

God asked me to quit my medical profession. Believe me; it was tough because I was making a lot of money; six digit figures every year. It was a very difficult proposition. How could I quit and lose all that money to stand in a rented building with less than 200 people to preach? But God said, "Leave it and follow me; put me first." He said, "I will take care of you." Leave your profession; stop your business; stop seeing patients – just follow me. Do you know what I did? I set a date. The first person I told was First Lady, Pastor Gladys. I said, "This is my last day of working. I'm going to have Jesus as my employer now."

The moment I made that decision, do you know what happened? A building came to fruition. It was like God was waiting for me to just say, "You know what, God, I'm going to put you first." The moment I put Him first, doors just opened and things moved quickly like a dream come true. At one point, I was waiting and I said, "God, I will only do that if I have everything put together – a building and church members. When everything is fine then I will quit." If I had kept on waiting for that day, we'd probably still be in the hotel room or at Merchant Square Mall trying to pay rent every month to keep the church going. But the moment that step was taken, things began to change miraculously. Clearly, putting God first releases supernatural provisions in your life.

Putting God first is not only being at church on time. It means putting God first in every area of your life. Can you do that or is it too hard to do? You may think, "I can't do that. My loved ones will say I don't love them." There was a minister I looked up to as a young man. His wife passed away. He was already scheduled to preach. Do you know, he still went to church that Sunday morning and preached before going back to handle the funeral arrangements for his wife. Do you think he was crazy? No. He made a commitment to put God first. Do you think God saw what he did? Yes.

I challenge you to put God first. Don't be like any other Christians. Let God be your all in all. The Bible says God is the Alpha and the Omega. He is the Beginning and the End. All the way in between, He's there. Some people say they can't attend church because they are sad. In other words, sadness comes before God.

Everything that is about God is God's. Some of us think putting God first means praying alone at home. But that's not true. If church has to do with God, that's part of God. If giving your tithe has to do with God, that's part of God. If showing love to your loved ones has to do with God, that is part of God.

God sees our hearts. The Bible says that God who sees your heart would reward you openly. He knows what you are thinking. He knows if you really want His presence or not. He knows if you are faking. Many times, you are sad but you pretend you are happy. You smile when you want to frown and laugh when you want to cry. You fake it. God knows you're pretending. The person next to you may not know you are pretending, but God knows. You cannot hide even your thoughts from Him. He knows what you are thinking. If you give someone a hug and say, "Oh, I love you sister. I love you," and in your heart, you wish the person dead, God knows it. You cannot fool him, so we must be very conscious of that.

## Obedience

The third principle that we learned from this particular scripture and Elijah's encounter with the widow is obedience. The woman was obedient. She did what the prophet asked her to do. The prophet told her, "Go fetch me water to drink." She did it. Prophet Elijah said, "Come back. Give me some food." She did it. What do you think would have been the outcome if she had disobeyed? Disobedience would have ruined the power of God in her life as it will do with yours. Disobedience will clog up the grace of God upon your life. If you really want God's power to flow continuously, you must obey His Word.

## Sharing the Anointing

If you want the anointing to increase then you have to share it.

> Now there cried a certain woman of the wives of the sons of the prophets unto Elisha, saying, Thy servant my husband is dead; and thou knowest that thy servant did fear the Lord: and the creditor is come to take unto him my two sons to be bondmen.
>
> And Elisha said unto her, What shall I do for thee? tell me, what hast thou in the house? And she said, Thine handmaid hath not anything in the house, save a pot of oil.
>
> Then he said, Go, borrow thee vessels abroad of all thy neighbours, even empty vessels; borrow not a few.
>
> And when thou art come in, thou shalt shut the door upon thee and upon thy sons, and shalt pour out into all those vessels, and thou shalt set aside that which is full.
>
> So she went from him, and shut the door upon her and upon her sons, who brought the vessels to her; and she poured out.
>
> And it came to pass, when the vessels were full, that she said unto her son, Bring me yet

a vessel. And he said unto her, There is not a vessel more. And the oil stayed.

Then she came and told the man of God. And he said, Go, sell the oil, and pay thy debt, and live thou and thy children of the rest.

And it fell on a day, that Elisha passed to Shunem, where was a great woman; and she constrained him to eat bread. And so it was, that as oft as he passed by, he turned in thither to eat bread.

And she said unto her husband, Behold now, I perceive that this is an holy man of God, which passeth by us continually.

Let us make a little chamber, I pray thee, on the wall; and let us set for him there a bed, and a table, and a stool, and a candlestick: and it shall be, when he cometh to us, that he shall turn in thither.

And it fell on a day, that he came thither, and he turned into the chamber, and lay there.

And he said to Gehazi his servant, Call this Shunammite. And when he had called her, she stood before him.

And he said unto him, Say now unto her, Behold, thou hast been careful for us with all this care; what is to be done for thee? Wouldest thou be spoken for to the king, or to the captain of the

host? And she answered, I dwell among mine
own people.

And he said, What then is to be done for her?
And Gehazi answered, Verily she hath no child,
and her husband is old.

And he said, Call her. And when he had called
her, she stood in the door (2 Kings 4:1–15).

Elisha asked the woman a pertinent question. "What do
you have in your house?" The answer would make all the
difference. She started, "I have nothing..." Her first three
words were daunting and a clear sign of her desperation and
desolation. However, she continued – "but." She said, "but a
little pot of oil." Interestingly, inspite of her dire situation, she
still saw the significance of the little oil she had.

In the Bible oil always signifies the anointing. On hearing
she still had a little oil left, Elisha knew God could do something with it. He said to the woman, "Go and borrow the
vessels abroad of all thy neighbors, even empty vessels.
Borrow not a few."

These are very strange instructions. It seems more logical
for the prophet to have told her, "Go borrow oil so you can
sell it and make a profit to pay the creditor." That would have
been a better idea. But he told her, "Go borrow vessels." Can
you imagine what might have gone through her thoughts?
*I'm telling you that the creditors are coming here to take my
sons for ransom. You are telling me to borrow empty vessels.
What will empty vessels do for me?*

Elijah had good reason for his request. Further, he told her
to pour the oil she had in the empty vessels she collected.
Again, this was illogical. How could the little oil she had fill
all those empty vessels she had collected? Yet. the woman

obeyed and the more she poured, the more the oil flowed. It only stopped when she ran out of vessels.

The principle is that if you want God's anointing on your life to flow, you have to share it. Pour it out. Give it out. Like this widow. Don't keep it to yourself. Release God's power on people when you meet them on the street. Let it go on your children and your neighbors. Release God's power on their lives.

Don't sit with what you've got whether it's little or much. Go out there and bring people to Christ. The more you win souls to Christ, the more God's anointing will be upon your life. Elijah on instructing the widow to shut herself in was advocating an important step to receiving and keeping the flow of the anointing. He understood the connection between having personal communion with God and the anointing. Essentially, we need to retreat from the busyness, the pressures, the concerns of life and go one-on-one with God. Be alone with Him and pray. God knows you are serious. He will not hesitate to let His power flow in your life ceaselessly.

# Conclusion

What do you want to do with this information you've received? If you have not yet accepted the free gift of forgiveness and eternal life that Jesus offers, you cannot have the anointing of the Holy Spirit. You can accept that free gift right now by repeating this simple prayer:

Dear Father, I come to You right now as a person who needs Jesus in my life. Thank You Jesus for dying for all my sins. I accept the free gift of forgiveness and eternal life that You offer. I confess with my mouth that Jesus is Lord, and I believe in my heart that He rose from the dead. Dear Jesus, come into my heart. Be my Lord and my Savior in Jesus' name. Amen.

If you have said this simple prayer, the Bible says that you are born again and on your way to live your best live ever.

The anointing is for you. Desire it! Go for it and walk in the power and anointing of the Holy Ghost. Do great exploits for the kingdom of God. You are anointed!

# About the author

Apostle Ese Duke is the founder and the General Overseer of Spirit Temple Bible Church. He is the President of Spiritual Father Apostolic Covering, providing spiritual and ministerial covering to leaders, ministries, and churches across the globe. He is also the founder, president, and rector of Spirit Temple Bible College with Headquarters based in Bethlehem PA. USA.

He is a man after God's heart, a dynamic preacher, and teacher of God's Word with an apostolic calling. He has made tremendous impact in the lives of people all across the world bringing the message of God's amazing love, grace, healing, and prosperity with a mandate from God according to Isaiah 61:1-2.

His ministry is characterized by the teaching of the awesome revelation of God's Word in simplicity and clarity, the move of God's power with tangible proofs of healing, miracles, signs, wonders, accurate word of knowledge and manifestations of prophetic declarations.

He is happily married to Reverend Gladys Duke, a co-laborer in the ministry and God's vineyard. They are blessed with six lovely and God-honoring children.